The Last Voyage of the Scotian

Also by Bill Freeman:

Shantymen of Cache Lake
The Bains Series 1, 1975

The Last Voyage of the Scotian
The Bains Series 2, 1976; re-issued 1998

First Spring on the Grand Banks
The Bains Series 3, 1983

Trouble at Lachine Mill
The Bains Series 4, 1983

The Harbour Thieves
The Bains Series 5, 1984

Danger on the Tracks
The Bains Series 6, 1987

Prairie Fire!
The Bains Series 7, 1998

The Last Voyage of the Scotian

Bill Freeman

James Lorimer & Company Ltd., Publishers
Toronto 1998

James Lorimer & Company acknowldeges the support of the Department of Canadian Heritage and the Ontario Arts Council in the development of writing and publishing in Canada. We acknowledge the support of the Canada Council for the Arts for our publishing program.

Canadian Cataloguing in Publication Data

Freeman, Bill, 1938 —
The Last Voyage of the Scotian

(Bains Series)
2nd ed.
ISBN 1-55028-644-7

I. Title.

PS8561.R378L3 1998 C813'.5'4 C98-932147-9
PR9199.3.F63L3 1998

James Lorimer & Company Ltd., Publishers
Egerton Ryerson Memorial Building
35 Britain Street
Toronto, Ontario
M5A 1R7

Printed and bound in Canada

Nova Scotia Song

The sun was setting in the west,
The birds were singing on ev'ry tree,
All nature seemed inclined for rest,
But still there was no rest for me.

REFRAIN:

Farewell to Nova Scotia, the sea bound coast!
Let your mountains dark and dreary be,
For when I am far away on the briny ocean tossed
Will you ever heave a sigh and a wish for me?

I grieve to leave my native land,
I grieve to leave my comrades all,
And my parents whom I held so dear,
And the bonny, bonny lass that I do adore.

The drums they do beat and the wars do alarm,
The captain calls, we must obey,
So farewell, farewell to Nova Scotia's charms,
For it's early in the morning I am far, far away.

I have three brothers and they are at rest,
Their arms are folded on their breast,
But a poor simple sailor just like me
Must be tossed and driven on the dark blue sea.

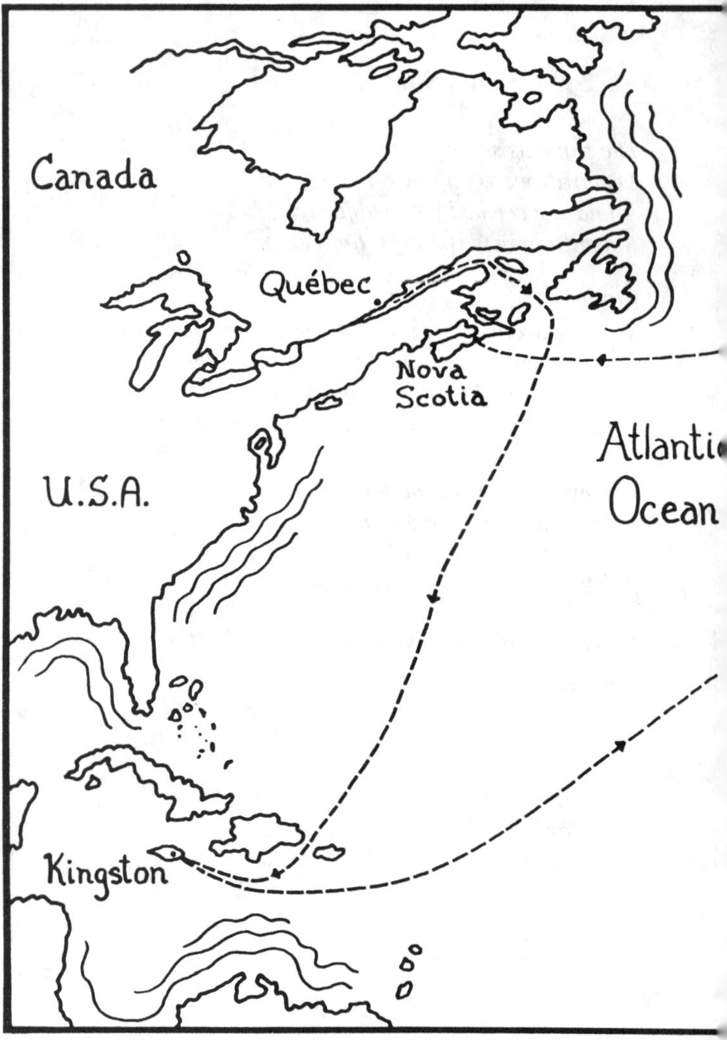

Canada
Québec
Nova Scotia
Atlantic Ocean
U.S.A.
Kingston

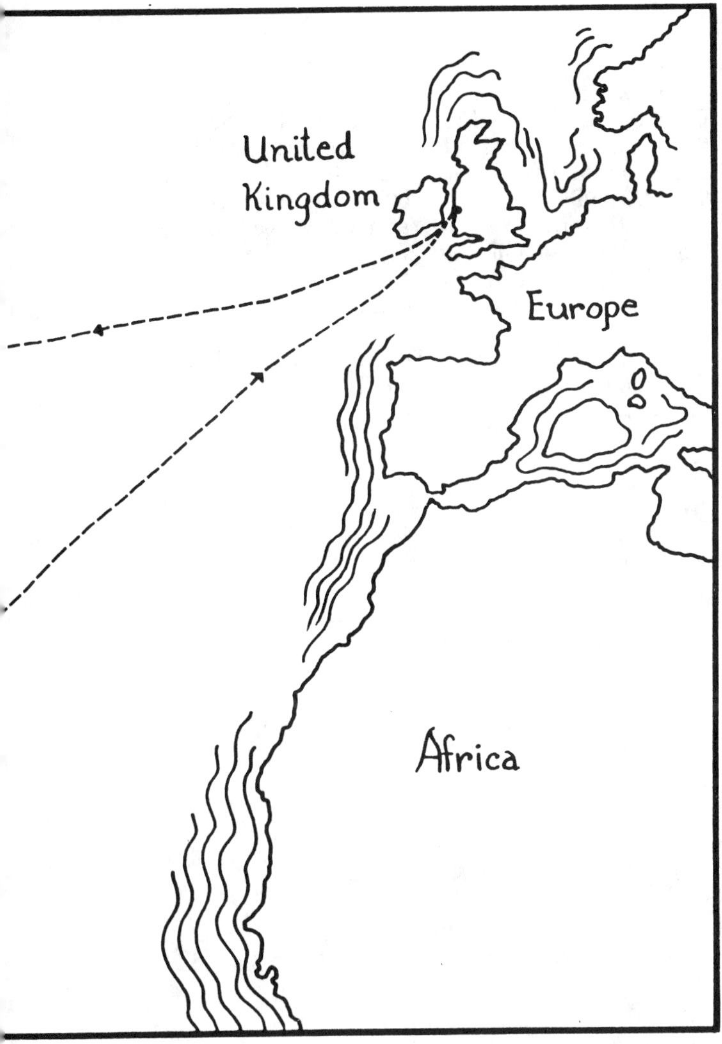
United
Kingdom
Europe
Africa

Photo credits

Dalhousie University Library, Halifax, Nova Scotia: 1, 2, 8, 10, 23. San Francisco Maritime Museum: 3. The National Maritime Museum, London: 4, 15, 17, 18, 19, 20, 21, 22. The Public Archives of Canada: 5, 6, 7. Yarmouth County Historical Society, Yarmouth, Nova Scotia: 9, 16. Notman Photographic Archives, McGill University, Montreal: 11, 13. Courtesy of the New Brunswick Museum: 12. The Illustrated London News, Elm House, London: 14.

Words for the *Nova Scotia Song* collected by Helen Creighton, copyright Gordon V. Thompson Limited, Toronto—used with permission.

CHAPTER 1

CRIMPS," the old raftsman had said to John and Meg Bains as they drifted into Québec City aboard the huge timber raft. "Crimps are all over this town. When those square-rigged sailing ships get into harbour, half the crew deserts. The only way a captain can get back to sea is to pay a crimp a month's wages for every seaman he can shanghai aboard. Now the two of you be careful when you get into that city or God knows what may happen."

But Meg and John were too excited to pay much attention to the warning. The year before, they had spent an eventful winter in a lumber shanty, and, after resting at home in Ottawa for a couple of weeks in early summer, had taken a job aboard a timber raft going to Québec City. Their experience had given them a sense of independence and strength beyond their years. Now was their chance to see the sights of the old French capital, and they felt they did not need anyone to warn them of dangers.

For six weeks they had drifted down the Ottawa and St. Lawrence Rivers and now, late in August, 1873, as the pilot shouted his orders to the crew, the enormous raft headed into one of the timber coves. Once it was tied up, the raftsmen scrambled around for their gear, pressed the foreman for their pay, and headed as quickly as possible for the taverns along Champlain Street.

Meg and John were as excited as the others, but before they set off on their tour, John insisted that they go right to the steamship office and book passage on a ship leaving the next day for Ottawa. They had been away from home for a long time and were anxious to spend the rest of the summer with their mother and younger brothers and sister. At last, with their chores done, they were free to do what they wanted.

Meg was excited. "Let's go up and see the fort." She was only thirteen and so high-spirited that at times her enthusiasm made her brother more than a little annoyed. She set off at a fast walk through the streets of Lower Town.

"Wait up!" said John impatiently. "If we walk like this, we'll be tired before we start." He was a sturdy fourteen-year-old, tall for his age, with thick, square-set shoulders. He lugged a canvas duffle bag over his back, and the two talked excitedly as they wove their way through the narrow streets.

It felt good to them to be finished with work and have the freedom to do what they wanted. Life in the bush and aboard the raft had been exciting in its own way, but the routine was monotonous. By contrast, the city was alive with variety. Rough sailors and shantymen were crowded into taverns; women dressed in long colourful gowns were out doing their shopping. Often John and Meg passed priests and nuns dressed in long black robes, and there were many businessmen wearing expensive cutaway coats and top hats. The city was a rough frontier town where men came to spend their money and have a good time. Even though the firm arm of the law was represented on each street corner by a big, blue-coated policeman, there was a restlessness about the place that could not be suppressed.

Finally, the two of them had wound their way through the thronged streets of Lower Town to the bottom of the stairs that led to the escarpment. Meg's excitement could be contained no longer. "Come on," she shouted. "I'll race you to the top!" She hitched up her long skirt, and with her blonde hair flowing behind, she took the steps two at a time. "Come on!" she shouted.

John's first thought was that Meg was being childish, but she was a younger sister and she was leaving him behind. Impulsively he took up the challenge, running as hard as he could, the duffle bag bouncing on his shoulder. Laughing excitedly, Meg kept in front, dodging between the people, but her long skirt was holding her back. John gained rapidly, taking three steps at a time and shouting at her to get out of the way. After running up three flights of stairs, John caught up to his sister, but as he surged ahead in the race, he suddenly bumped into a man coming out of a tavern. They collided with a tremendous jolt: John careened off balance and stumbled to his knees. The man had been given a good shaking, but had not fallen. "What do you think you're doing?" he asked angrily in English. He was thirty-five or forty, dressed in expensive, flashy clothes; his round, pink face was clean-shaven, except for the moustache that fringed his heavy upper lip. "You could hurt a person runnin' on these stairs."

"I'm sorry, sir." John picked himself off the ground, brushing his clothes as he spoke. "I didn't mean to do it."

"Well don't ever be doin' it again!" The man stood with his hands on his hips, his bowler hat pushed back on his head and his jacket open to expose a red waistcoat and a gold watch-chain. His pale eyes shifted from Meg to John, studying them closely. "Are you from around these parts?" he asked John.

John was eager to please in an attempt to make up for the accident he had. "No sir. We're from Ottawa. We've come down river on a log raft and we're going back home tomorrow."

Meg stood very still, suspiciously examining the man.

"Got any relatives here?" he asked.

"No sir."

The man's round, puffy face was flushed as if from heavy drinking. He seemed to be studying the situation for a long moment. "Well then, maybe I can give some help. Night is comin' on. Do you have a place to stay?"

Meg glanced anxiously at her older brother. They both felt distinctly uncomfortable, but John was reluctant to appear impolite. "No sir," he replied.

"Québec's not a safe place this time of year for young people like yourself. The sailors are in port and the raftsmen are down the river fillin' the taverns. You need a good place to stay. I'll help you."

John glanced at his sister with a feeling of unease. "No sir. That's nice of you, but we can find our own place."

"Don't be silly," said the man with a sudden show of friendship. "You're strangers to this town. No family, no relatives. It's the least I should do. Come along. I know just the right place."

Meg and John were tired now, and the strange city took on a menacing atmosphere in the darkness, which made them eager to be off the streets. They would have preferred to find a room by themselves, but the man was so polite and friendly that they could find no way to refuse.

"All right," John finally said. "That's good of you to offer."

The man smiled broadly, as if he had won a victory, and again John and Meg felt increasingly uneasy. But now there was little that they could do. Already the man had set off at a fast pace, forcing them both to hurry along behind.

They travelled through a labyrinth of narrow streets in Lower Town, dodging between sailors and raftsmen. From the taverns they could hear loud voices and singing. Periodically they caught glimpses of the tall rigging of sailing ships and the hulking forms of steamers tied up at docks nearby. Once, a drunk staggered out of a tavern and almost knocked Meg over, and while passing a dark alley they caught a glimpse of a group of men arguing in loud voices. But at no time did their companion pause. Meg and John hurried after him, holding back their fears.

Finally, they came to a three-story stone structure built in the colonial French style. It had a sign outside in English saying *The Three Sailors' Inn*. The windows were caked with dirt and the paintwork was peeling. The man walked up the stairs and entered without knocking. Meg and John cautiously followed, eyeing every detail.

Inside, a heavyset woman was standing behind a makeshift counter. John and Meg could see a number of men in another room dressed as sailors, drinking around tables. The place had a strong smell of putrid beer and alcohol. The dim light through the dingy windows showed the squalor of dirty cups and dishes on the tables, and scattered debris on the floor.

"I'd like you to give these two young people a room for the night. You can bill me. They're friends of mine." The man stood with his elbow on the counter and his hand on his hip as if he was familiar with the place.

Meg tried to show their independence. "We have money. We'll pay for our own room."

The man seemed pleased with himself. "If you want. I'm just tryin' to be of service to two youngsters alone in a big city." He pushed his bowler hat back on his head. Then, with an elaborate motion, he took out his gold watch from his waistcoat and examined it closely. "I must be going. I'm sure your trip to Québec City will be eventful."

After paying for the room and depositing their bag in it, John and Meg went back into the street for a quick tour of the city while there was still daylight. Their high spirits had given way to a disturbing sense of unease.

"Why do you think he did that?" Meg asked as they walked up the steps toward Upper Town.

"I don't know. Maybe he was just being nice."

"I don't think so."

"Why do you say that?" John asked with a hint of annoyance.

"It's just a feeling."

"Well he seemed all right to me."

"I just don't like it. I don't like any part of it."

"You're being silly." John wanted to set his younger sister at ease, but he felt a nervousness of his own.

The climb to Upper Town was tiring and they had to rest for a few moments before setting off again. When they finally got to the fort, they climbed up the walls and sat on the battlements overlooking the river.

It was a magnificent view. The fort had been built at the highest point of the escarpment so that it could dominate the whole area. Here the river was narrow and fast flowing. Downstream, to the east, they could see the green island of Orléans surrounded by deep blue waters. Upstream, to the west, the timber coves stretched as far as they could see. The coves were jammed with huge timber rafts, and tied up alongside them were the square-rigged timber droghers taking on cargo.

Québec City was the commercial heart of the Canadian timber trade. From July through to the end of September, the squared timber rafts would arrive from the upper Ottawa River Valley. The big windjammers would come up the St. Lawrence from the North

Atlantic during this time to take on cargo destined for the British ports of Liverpool, Glasgow or occasionally the West Indies.

Virtually all of those ships had a British registry, although many came from Canadian ports in Nova Scotia and New Brunswick. They carried cargo in both directions. The ships went to Britain with their holds filled with timber and returned across the North Atlantic with their between-decks filled with machinery, manufactured goods or steerage emigrants seeking a new life. It was here, at Québec City, that most of the new Canadians made their first landfall in the New World.

As Meg and John sat on the ramparts of the old fort, the sun slowly began to set behind the dark hills in the distance.

"Do you really think the sea captains use crimps to get sailors, John?" asked Meg, remembering what the old raftsman had said. "I mean, do you think that there are people who steal sailors and put them aboard ships?"

The darkness of the night was quickly coming upon them, and the river below seemed like a dark winding ribbon. The spider-web rigging of the masts of the windjammers could barely be made out as the ships bobbed in the current.

John listened without a word as his sister spoke. "It seems strange to me," she continued. "Think of it. You could be anyone, and then a crimp comes along, and the next thing you know you're at sea on a ship. Well, I'd like to see them try it with us," she said firmly. "We'd show them, wouldn't we, John?"

Her brother said nothing, thinking of the tough faces and strong arms of the sailors they had seen in the streets. Below them, the city had turned into a jumble of dark forms, lit with an occasional flicker from a coal oil lantern or a candle. A seaport was a dangerous place at night. He sat up, as if coming out of a dream, and said, "Come on. We'd better get back to the inn."

They made their way from the ramparts and walked uncertainly through the streets of Upper Town. It was pitch black among the buildings, except for a few lighted windows, and John and Meg both felt a growing sense of fear as they made their way through the shadowy, unfamiliar streets.

Finally, they found the top of the stairs, and as they went down the steps they held hands for reassurance. Once, a drunken sailor brushed by and John grabbed Meg's arm in panic. At last they made it into Lower Town. Here, it was a little lighter. Gaslights at every corner, the lanterns of people passing in the streets, as well as the light from the tavern and hotel windows, helped brighten the darkness. They hurried on, anxious to find some place where they could feel safe, until finally they made it back to the inn.

But the inside of their hotel seemed darker than the street. A single candle burned on the counter, casting dark shadows in the corners of the hallway. In the room set aside for drinking a fire glowed on the hearth, revealing ten or twelve men sitting around tables. There was a quiet hush about the place.

John and Meg waited at the counter for the woman to give them a candle to guide them to their room. As they stood there, a tall, heavyset man of about forty-five emerged from the bar. He was dressed in the manner of sea captains in a blue double-breasted coat, lined with brass buttons. On his head was a peaked cap. He had a full black beard with iron-grey streaks, but in the dim light, all John and Meg could see of his face were dark steady eyes set in a pale forehead.

The man addressed John directly. "I am Cap'n Barnard of the ship *Scotian*. I heard you're a bright lad who has been in the lumber shanty. I'd like to offer you a berth on my ship, and I'd promise to give you an apprenticeship. The pay would be five dollars a month. We sail for the Indies at dawn."

The boy was completely taken back with the unexpected offer. "I … I don't think I could, sir." He was stammering. "You see I have my mother to help support, and my younger brothers and sister. I couldn't go away on a ship and leave them."

The captain's face tightened, and the lines of his mouth turned down into a deep scowl. "I'm desperate for a crew. I have to cast off in the morning and I still need one more for my complement. Sign on with me!" He seemed to bark out the words as if shouting an order to his crew.

"No sir. I can't. I've my family to think of."

Suddenly the round-faced man who had brought them to the inn was standing in the doorway. Beside him was the woman innkeeper and in the background two men dressed as sailors.

John and Meg glanced anxiously at each other. "Please," said John quietly. "Could we have a candle to go up to our room?"

For a moment the woman stared at them blankly. Then, producing a candle from a small drawer, she lit it from the one on the counter and gave it to the boy. John led the way up the long creaking staircase, holding the flame high to show the way. Halfway up, Meg glanced back to see the sinister group, still gathered in the pale light, silently watching them. An involuntary shudder of fear went through her body.

"Lock the door," she whispered once they were in the room. "I don't like the looks of those people."

John put the candle in the holder and then turned the key that was in the lock. "Don't get worried, Meg," he said, trying to reassure his sister, but he was frightened himself.

The two sat on the bed trying to collect themselves. In the dim light they could see that the room was small and dirty and almost bare of furniture.

Suddenly, there was a creak on the stairs. Then there was the sound of footsteps. Meg and John gripped each other's hand. The sounds came nearer and louder. Now they were at the top of the landing.

There was a pounding at the door. "Who … who is it?" John asked with fear in his voice.

The woman innkeeper replied through the door. "I've some tea for you."

Meg and John looked at each other, relieved. "Just a moment," said Meg, as she turned the lock and opened the door. All five people were there. Meg shrieked.

"Grab the boy!" someone shouted. "Quick, before he gets away!" The two rough-looking sailors rushed inside, caught the startled boy and forced him to the floor with his arm pinned behind his back. All John could do was give a short painful scream.

"Close the door," came the order from the round-faced man who was obviously in charge. "We've got to get him to sign this contract."

Meg had been completely ignored. She stood in the corner, watching in horror as her brother was subdued by the two men. Finally she reacted. "Stop it! Leave him alone! Let him go!" She screamed and then tried to rush to John's aid.

"Get her!" yelled their leader. "Ouch, you demon!" Meg had hit him in the stomach with her elbow. "Grab her!" There was a fierce struggle. The woman innkeeper joined and within a moment the two of them had subdued the young girl with their superior strength.

"Hold her," he said to the woman. "She's a devil, that one."

The man released his grip on Meg and stood up. He took a paper from his pocket, unfolded it, and went to where John was being held by the two men. "You sign this paper, my boy, and then ship out aboard the *Scotian* with Cap'n Barnard."

John struggled vainly. "You're a crimp, aren't you?"

A broad smile slid across the man's face. "You're a smart one to figure that out. You'll do well aboard ship."

"No, never!" John struggled, but the weight of the two men pinned him down. One of them took his left arm and bent it behind his back, then pushed it until an agonizing pain shot up through his shoulder.

"You'll sign this paper, boy. Then we'll let you go."

"No I can't. I've got to go home. My family …."

But they wrenched his arm so hard that the words were replaced by cries of pain.

"Sign boy, and that'll be the end of it. You'll get paid while you're aboard." The crimp stood over him with the paper and pencil in hand. "Sign!"

"No!" John struggled against the man's grip, but it was useless. His arm was twisted even further behind his back and the pain shot through his shoulder and into his chest.

"Sign!" said the crimp angrily.

The pain was even sharper this time. His arm felt close to breaking.

"You'll sign boy, even if we have to break your arm to do it." The crimp put the paper in front of John and, taking his free hand, guided it along to make a few scratches. "There, that'll do. It's done. Let him go."

John collapsed, close to losing consciousness.

"There's your contract, Cap'n, and your seaman. Though God knows if he'll be much use to you."

The captain's eyes shifted from person to person. "Good, take him down to the *Scotian*. I'll pay you only when he's aboard."

Meg was finally able to shake herself free from the woman's grasp. "Are you really taking my brother, captain?" she asked in disbelief.

The master's face was stern. "He signed on fair and legal. The paper's there for all to see."

"That's not true. The crimp forced him to sign. You saw him."

"The boy's coming with me and that's the end of it."

"But you can't take him and leave me behind," she pleaded. "What will I do? Take me along with you."

"I don't need a girl aboard my ship. You'd just be in the way."

"Please Captain! I'm a good worker. Maybe I could help the cook."

"I won't have women aboard a ship of mine. They're just a nuisance."

Nothing made Meg more annoyed than to be rejected merely because she was a girl. After all, when she was in the shanty she had always worked as hard as her brother. "It's just not fair," she said, her eyes flashing. "You can't steal my brother. I'll go to the police."

"No one would believe you."

Meg looked desperately to each person. John had got to his feet now, but in spite of his struggles he was still firmly held in an arm-lock by the crimp's men. How could she free him? What was she to do? In an instant she had made up her mind. She made a sudden lunge for the door, tore it open and in a moment was running down the stairs.

"Grab her!" the crimp shouted. "Get her before she gets away!" He was into the hall with the woman right behind him. Their feet pounded loudly on the stairs and there were shouts. "Get her! Stop that girl!"

At the same time John struggled against his two captors with all his strength. "Leave me alone! Let me go!" He poked at them with his free hand and kicked at their shins, but within moments, the two crimp's men had pushed him down to the floor and had pinned his arm behind his back again.

There was noise on the stairs and the crimp came back into the room. His round face was deep red, his clothes were rumpled, and he was angry. "She got away. She disappeared around the corner, the little demon. Let's get this boy aboard ship before anything else happens," he said to the captain. "I'll deal with that girl when I catch her."

On the street John was closely guarded. The crimp walked in front of him, with the captain and his two men on either side, clutching his wrists. They went through back alleys, and all that John could see were ghost-like buildings outlined in the swaying lantern light. His arm throbbed with pain and his wrists hurt from the vice-like grip of the crimp's men. He smelled salt water now and was terrified at the prospect of being thrown aboard a strange ship, heading for an unknown port and an unknown fate. What would happen to his mother and the rest of the family? Where was Meg? Could she get help, or would the crimp and his men find her eventually?

As they came to the wharf's edge, a sliver of a moon gleamed on the water's surface, outlining the dark hulks of square-rigged ships which bobbed in the current. In a final, determined effort, John struggled to break away, but someone brutally wrenched his arm and a hand was clapped over his mouth to stifle any screams. He could only stand there helplessly, listening to the low, gruff conversation of the men and the lapping sound of the waves against the dock.

CHAPTER 2

AFTER a long wait, John was pushed roughly up a gangplank to the deck of a big windjammer. The moon faintly outlined the small group of men and the surface of the water sparkled brilliantly in the light, but the deck itself was dark and gloomy. "Put the boy in the steward's cabin," John heard the captain whisper, and the crimp's men forced him along to a door in the aft section of the ship. Then he was thrust into complete blackness as the door slammed and a bolt shot into place on the outside.

For a moment it was deathly quiet. Then John heard the captain say, "Come into my cabin. Once you get your money, I want you crimps off my ship."

"Remember, Cap'n, you're in this as much as any of us ...." was all he could hear of the crimp's reply, and then there was silence.

The boy remained motionless for a long time. The pain where his arms had been twisted was intense, but as he moved, some of the stiffness began to ease. Suddenly he sat upright, acutely aware of the seriousness of his situation. He was trapped aboard a square-rigged sailing ship that was obviously about to cast off on some unknown voyage. But where was Meg? His mother had made him responsible for his sister's safety.

The boy got to his feet and fumbled with the door handle, but it would not open. He shook it in a rage and then pounded on the heavy oak panels. "Let me out! Let me out!" he shouted. "You can't hold me like this." He slammed his fists harder and harder against the door until his hands ached. "Let me out! I've got to get free!"

After a couple of minutes he stopped to listen. There was nothing but absolute silence outside. It was as if the ship was deserted. Again he pounded rhythmically on the door and shouted with all his might: "Let me out! You can't take me like this!"

He stopped to listen, but there was no sound anywhere.

What could he do? He slumped onto the floor beside the door and tried to think things through clearly. There seemed to be no way that anyone aboard ship was going to listen to him. His only hope of getting ashore was Meg. Maybe she could persuade the police to come and free him.

In a final effort he got to his feet and began pounding on the door again. "Help, help!" he shouted. "Let me out of here!" For at least two minutes he pounded, but gradually his efforts slowed and stopped. There was nothing but silence outside. John felt a desperate sense of isolation and terror. He was trapped and there was nothing that he could do to help himself.

He sank onto the floor beside the door and listened. Every bone and muscle in his body ached, and his mind kept turning over and over an endless series of worries. How would his mother support herself while he was away? Could his thirteen-year-old sister survive in a strange city without money or friends? If he was going to be shanghaied, how long would he be at sea? Would he ever return?

Slowly his exhaustion overcame him and he drifted off to sleep, huddled by the door of the steward's cabin.

He had no idea how long he had been lying there, when he heard a noise outside the door. He sat bolt upright and listened. The sound was faint at first but then it got louder. "John, John, where are you? Where are you? Answer me, please!"

It was Meg. She had found him. "I'm in here!" he whispered excitedly.

There was silence for a moment. "Is that you, John?"

"Yes, I'm locked in the cabin, Meg." He was talking loudly now. "The door is bolted from the outside."

"I can hear you." She seemed to be groping, but suddenly the iron bolt slid back and the door was opened.

"John, I'm so glad to find you," Meg whispered. "I was so frightened. I've been searching for so long, I thought that you were gone forever."

"Come in quickly, Meg, before anyone sees you." John closed the door and they sat on the floor in the inky black cabin. "What happened, Meg? Tell me all about it."

"I was scared. You have no idea. I ran down the streets until I was sure that I was away from the crimp. It was awful. The streets were filled with men and women but none of them paid any attention to me. Finally I found a policeman and I told him what had happened, but he wouldn't believe that you'd been shanghaied. All he asked was whether you'd signed the contract, and when I said yes, he wouldn't do anything. He said that you'd signed on legally and there wasn't anything he could do. So I went to find another policeman, but he wouldn't do anything either. It was terrible. I went to find the police station, but I got lost." Meg was shaking with anger as she recounted her story. "I didn't know what to do, John. No one would help me. But then I remembered the name of the ship, the *Scotian.* So I came down to the wharf and I looked at every ship until finally I found it. I had to wait the longest time out on the dock. There was someone on deck and I could see him pacing back and forth, but finally he went away and so I came aboard." The young girl was shivering now from the cold and her own fear.

"You've done well, Meg. I was so worried about you. They wouldn't let me go. They held onto me every step of the way and then put me in this cabin and locked it from outside. There was no way I could get out." John was feeling stronger and more confident. There was hope now that Meg had found him. "Let's wait a few minutes to rest up. Then we can sneak off the ship."

They both tried to relax, but they had been thoroughly frightened and they listened to every sound out on the deck. Finally John stood up. "We've got to go now, Meg, before it gets light." He groped for the door handle, turned it, and slowly eased it open. Cautiously, he put his head out of the opening. Already the dawn was beginning to grey the sky to the east so that things could be seen clearly on deck.

Suddenly he withdrew his head in panic and closed the door. "There's someone on deck, Meg! He's standing by the gangway."

"What'll we do?"

"I don't know. We've got to get off this ship. If it sets sail with us aboard, we're trapped!"

"Maybe we can make a run for it?"

"No, we'd never get down the gangway and the deck is too high off the wharf for us to jump."

"Then we're trapped."

"Let's wait, Meg. Keep calm. Maybe there'll be a chance."

But the two of them were far from keeping calm. Both knew that this was their only chance to get back home.

A few moments later, John eased the door open again. The dawn was very close. Red streaks of morning filled the sky. Within minutes it would be daylight. Cautiously, the boy poked his head out and again withdrew quickly. "There's two of them now, Meg. It's the captain, I think. What are we to do?"

There was a commotion outside. "All hands on deck!" the captain shouted at the top of his voice. Within moments they could hear the sound of running feet. "Hans, take the helm. Stand by to cast off forward and aft lines. Look smart about it."

"What are we going to do?" Meg whispered urgently.

"Hide, Meg. Hide until we're out at sea. Then at least we can stay together."

Suddenly the door was flung open and the captain stood peering into the dark room, the bright rays of sun behind him.

"Who left this door unlocked?" he shouted over his shoulder to the crew on deck.

Meg cowered back into the shadows, afraid to face the captain, and John stepped forward into the cool morning air to shield her.

"Step smartly, boy. I won't have any laggards aboard my ship." The captain studied John keenly. "Well, at least you're a strong one. Now to work with you, and be quick at it."

John shut the door behind him and hurried off with the other man. In the brilliant sunlight, he saw a smoky mist rising from the river, and the tall masts of the ships like a winter forest rising on either side, swaying gently in the current. Above them the city of Québec clung to its great rock.

The captain paced the deck of his ship, impatiently waiting for enough sailors to turn out before issuing his orders. At last he was satisfied. "Cast the lines off forward," he shouted in his gruff voice. The heavy rope was loosened. A stevedore on the dock freed it from the stanchion and threw his end into the water. Three sailors pulled it aboard, hand over hand, and coiled it neatly on the foredeck. The prow of the ship gently drifted away from the wharf.

"Cast off aft!" barked the captain. Again the rope was loosened, and another group of sailors pulled it aboard. The ship drifted away from the wharf and out into the current of the St. Lawrence.

"Set your course to the starboard of that buoy in the channel, helmsman," the captain shouted. "Set the jibs! Set the main mizzen sail!"

Two sailors ran forward to set the three jibs, and three ran to the poop deck. They loosened a rope which led through a series of blocks, then arranged themselves in a line and began heaving with every ounce of their strength.

The captain suddenly saw John standing idle at the rail amidships. "Get up here boy!" he shouted angrily. "I won't have any member of my crew hanging about while there's work to be done." He made a threatening gesture as if he would cuff the boy.

John ran to the other men, and grabbing the end of the rope, began pulling with all the strength in his back and legs. "Heave!" someone shouted, and the sailors gave an extra surge of power on the rope. "Heave!" came the shout again. John felt awkward. His feet seemed to get in the way; his arms and back were aching from the rough treatment he had received, and the rope burned into his hands. "Heave!" came the shout again and slowly the sail on the mizzenmast unfurled into a broad stretch of canvas.

The captain waited to feel how the ship would react. Slowly the north wind filled the huge sail, tilting the ship slightly over on its starboard beam. The *Scotian* moved imperceptibly at first, then gathered speed, and the clipper bow began to slice through the water into the middle of the current.

Captain Barnard, standing near the mizzenmast, waited until the ship was in just the right position. "Ten degrees to larboard," he shouted to the helmsman. "Follow the buoys out to the open water."

They were in mid-channel now, with the wind off the larboard beam pushing them through the water at a speed of three or four knots. Québec City, with its fort perched high over the river, was slowly dwindling behind them. A bright enormous sun had risen just above the horizon, bringing the warmth of a new day.

"Mr. Mckenzie!" shouted the captain. "Get the rest of those lazy laggards out of the fo'c's'le and assemble the crew at midships."

"Aye, sir."

A number of the crew members were already on deck but many of them were still in the forecastle, the sailors' quarters, sleeping off the effects of nights of strenuous drinking in port. Mr. Mckenzie, the youthful mate, and Mr. Ryerson, the bosun, made their way forward to the door of the forecastle.

Mr. Mckenzie stood at the entrance. "All hands on deck!" he shouted. "All hands on deck and look lively about it." Within a few moments, two sailors appeared and then a third. The officers waited for a minute and then disappeared below.

The others standing at midships could hear some of the shouting. "Get yourself out there, you drunken sailor!" Then a moment later, "Get moving before I tan your hide with a rope's end."

Gradually the sailors came out on deck in ones and twos. They squinted their eyes into the harsh morning sunlight and then hurried midships to join the others before anything else happened to them. The last to emerge was a tall, broad-shouldered man with light sandy hair. He was in his late twenties, slim but powerful, towering over the mate and the bosun who followed behind. His face was angular with a square chin and a sharp nose. He was clean shaven and had the dark windburned look of a man who worked out-of-doors for long hours. Even from a distance John could see that he was angry. His face was set in a hard scowl and, in spite of the shouts of the mate, he moved as slowly as possible to show his open defiance of authority.

The captain was pacing back and forth in front of the men, impatient to get on with the "outward-bound" speech that was traditionally given to new crews. The sailors looked a ragged bunch, dressed in rough clothing and peaked caps much like any other working men who lived in the city. They were of all ages and nationalities. Half of them seemed to be still drunk or drugged, uncertain of where they were or what had happened to them. But, in spite of this, they were a hearty-looking group of men, long used to hardships.

"I want you to listen carefully," said the captain from his position against the rail. "My name, for those who just signed on, is Cap'n Barnard and this is the ship *Scotian*. She's a nine-hundred-and-sixty-ton clipper loaded with squared timber. We're outward bound for Jamaica in the West Indies. Let me warn you that this is no lime-juice gentleman's ship. The registry is Yarmouth, Nova Scotia, and any man who's been to sea knows the reputation of the Bluenose fleet. We run the tightest ships under sail. All members of the crew from able seaman to the boy work a full day or you'll be gettin' the taste of a rope across yer back. When I shout an order I want you to snap to it. If you settle down and do your work, then we'll have a good voyage. If not, then my officers and I will make short shrift of you. Do you understand?"

The captain paused, trying to judge the effect of his words, but the men seemed impassive. John could see that words meant little to the crew without some action to back them up. Only the tall, heavyset man who had been the last to come out of the forecastle seemed at all interested.

"We'll be dividing the crew into two watches," began the captain again. "I will be handling the first watch, and the mate here, Mr. Mckenzie, will be handling the second. The bosun is Mr. Ryerson. He knows more about the sea than any of the rest of us added together, and it'll be his job to supervise the deck work."

The captain paused for a moment, looking at his crew. "I'll whip you men into sailors within a matter of days. So let me warn you. Either buckle down to my discipline or you'll be a sorry lot. Do you understand?"

As the captain spoke the tall sailor seemed to get increasingly angry. Finally, he could hide his feelings no longer. "I want to know, Cap'n, why you set the crimps onto us?"

"You were signed on fair and legal."

"I was drunk," the angry sailor shouted. "You got some crimp to get me drunk. Then he slipped me a mickey finn and dumped me aboard. I woke up and we're out in the channel heading for the open sea. I don't want this! I want to choose my own passage!"

"That's right," another sailor said and three or four others were nodding their heads in agreement.

The captain came toward the big man. His face was grim as if expecting a fight. "What's your name?" he ordered.

"Canso is what they call me. I hail from the same place in Nova Scotia."

"What's your rank?"

"Able seaman."

The captain was within arm's reach of Canso now. He stood a hand shorter, but his shoulders were just as broad. The two men glared at each other. "Are you intent on being a troublemaker on this voyage, Canso?"

"I say you shanghaied me aboard this ship, Cap'n. Not only me but half the rest of this crew. I tell you it's not fair. We should be put ashore downriver."

The captain stood his ground. "You're on a Nova Scotian ship, Canso. You should know what that means. You'll take orders from me even if I have to beat it into you. This ship will not be run from the fo'c's'le!"

"I don't want to sail aboard some stinking wooden-hulled ship that's so rotten she's ready to sink. You shanghaied me aboard with your crimps. I'll not work under conditions like that!"

"Seize him!" shouted the captain to his officers. "We'll clap you in irons for a couple of days and then we'll see what you say!"

Canso clenched his fists and crouched down as the three officers closed in on him. He seemed as intent on winning his point as the captain was to enforce his discipline. But then suddenly he seemed to give up. "Put me in irons. What difference does it make? A sailor is a prisoner anyway."

John could see that Canso's anger had turned quickly into despair, and he began to realize how hopeless the situation was. If this strong, young seaman could be so totally defeated by the captain, what possible hope could there be for him and his younger sister?

Captain Barnard did not miss the opportunity to show the rest of the crew that his authority must be unquestioned. "Take him to the hold. And let this be a lesson to every sailor here. I'll not have mutiny aboard this ship. Any man who tries will receive worse than Canso!"

The mate led Canso away and the captain glanced up at the rigging. "The current's slacking and we'll soon need sails for the St. Lawrence," he told his officers. Then, as if in an afterthought, he shouted down to the crew, "Stand by to set sails!"

During this time, Meg had been standing at the door of the steward's cabin listening to the activities on the main deck. She had known all along that as soon as they were into the channel, she would have to reveal herself. This seemed like the best opportunity. Casually, she opened the door and walked over to her brother John who was lounging against the rail.

From his position up on the poop deck the captain saw her but it took him a moment to react. Then in a rush he scrambled down the ladder and stormed across the deck to where John and Meg were standing. His anger was frightening. "You're his sister!" he shouted. "Why are you aboard this ship?"

But Meg faced him with her hands on her hips and a look of defiance. “I’m going to come on this voyage. You can’t keep me away.”

“But … but I don’t need a young girl on this ship. I told you I didn’t want you.”

“You won’t give me a chance, Captain.”

The master seemed huge, towering before the young girl and her brother. “I should throw you both into the hold with the rats. This is insolence. How can I possibly get you off my ship now that we’re in mid-channel?”

“Well, you shouldn’t have stolen my brother,” she replied with equal anger.

“Meg, Meg, be careful,” John whispered, worried that his sister’s impulsiveness would get them into even more trouble.

“I haven’t time for this monkey business,” the captain stormed, pacing away. “The ship is in the channel and there’s not a moment to lose. We must set sail.”

He called out a loud order, and sailors on every side began to spring into the rigging, scrambling up the shrouds to the topgallant yards.

The *Scotian* was a three-masted ship. The two forward masts were square-rigged, each with five big sails of canvas, while the mizzenmast at the aft of the ship carried three square sails at the top and a big schooner-type sail at the bottom. The crew began setting sails at the top and worked their way down.

John and Meg stood on the deck watching the others, uncertain what to do. Suddenly the captain was shouting, “You, boy, move! Get up into that rigging or

I'll tan your backside." In a moment John was into the main shrouds, slowly climbing up past the main yards, straining to follow the others.

Meg was uncertain what to do. She was still wearing her dress, but she did not want to be left behind. She was about to follow her brother, when the captain shouted at her.

"You don't think you're going up there?" he asked in disbelief.

"I can do anything my brother can do."

"Not aboard my ship, missy. You may think yourself very smart, but you'll buckle down to my discipline or tell a sorry tale." His eyes narrowed in anger. "I can't put you ashore now, but you'll work while you're on this ship. That I'll assure you." His finger wagged in her face. "Now get yourself aft and help the cook."

Meg was disappointed that she could not go up into the rigging, but at that moment John would have given anything to trade places with her. Once above deck, the wind, which had seemed so quiet, tugged at his clothing and whipped through the confusion of ropes, masts and yardarms. The higher he climbed, the more the ship swayed and the more unsteady he became.

Finally he made it to the topgallant yard where five men were already setting the royal sail. One of the sailors shouted to him, indicating that he should go out onto the larboard side of the yard to help. Carefully, he followed the others, putting his foot into the footropes and sliding it across to the stirrup. He held grimly onto the yardarm with one hand and tried to use the other to help unfurl the sail. Suddenly the heavy canvas came loose and flapped violently in the wind as it billowed full of air. John was flung against the yard, the force almost throwing him from his perch.

The boy looked beneath him. The sea was a hundred feet down and the waves were tossing the ship rhythmically. For the first time he realized that the masts were swaying from side to side as the ship pitched up into the waves and then fell into the troughs. One moment the yard he was perched on was over the sea on the larboard side, and the next moment, it was over on starboard. John was terrified. He was sure that he would be hurled far out into space and into the sea below. It was more than he could stand. His stomach turned and he clung desperately onto the rigging to save himself from plunging below.

The sailors had finished tying down the sail and were now scrambling back into the shrouds to go down to the next yardarm. John was in the way of the seamen on the larboard arm. Suddenly, one of them was shouting at him above the wind. "Get back into the shrouds!" But the boy did not move. Terror had frozen him to the spot.

The sailor was a young Englishman who spoke in a broad west country accent. "Get back!" he shouted angrily. "If ye cannot do the work of a sailor then get yerself below."

But John seemed paralysed. The seaman cursed and climbed over the boy, working his way down to the yard below. Other sailors followed, leaving John alone holding tightly to the ropes. John clenched his teeth and breathed in deep gulps of air to fend off panic. He tried to drive the swaying and lurching of the ship out of his mind, and somehow began to inch his way back to the shrouds. Slowly and painfully, he climbed back to the deck. When he finally made it, he was close to exhaustion, but quickly he had to scramble for the rail in order to vomit into the sea.

As he looked up, an angry Captain Barnard was standing beside him. "Get below," the master shouted scornfully. "You're useless as a seaman. What a mistake it was to even think of bringing you along. Go and help your sister in the galley."

CHAPTER 3

JOHN and Meg slowly worked their way toward the galley through the passages of the ship. The captain had made them both feel so humiliated that they did not even want to speak about it.

"Why is it that the two of ye can be so long in the mouth?" asked a small barrel-chested man who stood in a doorway. He had a big black handlebar moustache, and wore a long white apron and a bowler hat to cover what looked to be a completely bald head. To John and Meg he spoke with a strange, broad cockney accent. "'As the cap'n driven the sailor out of thee already?"

Meg could not help but smile. "Are you the cook?"

"Aye, Mr. Pepper is what they call me."

"The captain sent us below to help you," John said glumly.

"I saw you up in the riggin' there boy. It's not much of a sailor that you are. Well, if the old man sent you down 'ere it won't be for you to sit, I'll tell you that. The two of you are to look lively 'cause there'll be some hungry sailors comin' for their mess just as soon as them sails are set." Mr. Pepper spoke with a sharp edge to his voice, but there was something warm and friendly in his bright blue eyes.

"We've got a hard drivin' bucko cap'n there. 'E's a Bluenoser and they're the worst of the lot. 'E'll get the work out of you or tan yer backside with the end of a rope. So get yerself a movin.' You there — girl — set the table, and boy, you get into the galley and start stirrin' the gruel. Just as soon as them sailors get into the mess, you start fillin' bowls and servin' up hardtack as fast as you can."

Mr. Pepper leaned back against the door jam, his bowler hat perched on the back of his head and his moustache quivering as he critically watched the two Bains children begin their work. It was not long before the five seamen of the captain's watch came bursting into the mess and sat down. Meg hustled to serve them, knowing that Mr. Pepper was keeping a close watch.

They were a mixed assortment of men drawn from any port where a ship might make a landfall. There was a young Englishman from Bristol called Scobie, and a Portuguese sailor named Piedro. Hans was from Holland, Joseph from Poland, and Georges from Greece. They were all hung over from the wild nights they had spent in port and two of them, Scobie and Hans, were still suffering from the effects of a knockout drug called a mickey finn. When Meg carried in the steaming bowls of gruel, it seemed to her as if they were talking in a mad jumble of accents.

The oatmeal and flour gruel sweetened with molasses was served along with strong black tea and dried hardtack biscuits. The sailors all seemed annoyed but Hans was the most outspoken. "Do we not even have fresh food the first day out of port?"

"'Tis not fit for a dog," added Georges.

It was as if Mr. Pepper was waiting for the first sign of dissatisfaction. "If it's trouble you want, you'll get it from me. I'll skewer the first man who complains with my paring knife."

"But this is terrible stuff."

"Silence!" the cook shouted. "The man who speaks will be scrubbin' out my galley."

The sailors were wary and turned back to their food. They knew that if they made an enemy of the cook, their voyage could quickly turn into a miserable affair.

When the captain's watch had finished eating and went up on deck, the three sailors from the mate's watch came into the mess. There was Tommy, a small Englishman from Bristol, who was Scobie's friend; José, a black Cuban of about twenty-five, and Santana, a young Portuguese sailor. Already they had heard of Mr. Pepper's reputation from the men on the other watch and they were not about to put the cook to a test.

During the next few days, Meg and John got to know Mr. Pepper only too well. In his galley he acted like a tyrant, ordering the two of them about with shouted demands. But in spite of his gruff manner and the granite-like expression on his face, there was always humour in his eyes and a sly poking fun in his voice.

Their jobs were unending. They had to help prepare the meals and wash the mountains of dishes left behind. The officers' clothes had to be washed, and they were even relegated to cleaning out the cabins. The one chore they hated most of all was looking after the chickens. Six hens were kept in wooden cages to provide the crew with fresh eggs. Every day they had to be hauled out on deck for fresh air and fed grain and table scraps. Collecting the eggs was the worst part, because when John and Meg reached inside the cages, they ran the risk of having the bad-tempered birds give them sharp, painful pecks.

They felt humiliated to be given such lowly jobs, but still they found shipboard life fascinating. The *Scotian* was a wooden-hulled three-masted ship built in Nova Scotia. She was of clipper design, sharp-bowed and narrow in the beam to give speed. When the British and American ships took over the fast passenger runs, she had been converted into a bulk carrier and for years had sailed anywhere her captain could get a cargo.

Often Meg and John would go out on deck to peel potatoes or wash clothes so they could watch what was going on. Captain Barnard seemed to be always on deck. He paced back and forth near the helmsman with a worried look as if reluctant to delegate responsibility for steering the ship to anyone else. The other two officers, Mr. Mckenzie and Mr. Ryerson, worked the sailors hard while they were on watch. The crew adapted to their new command as if the officers meant little to them, and in spite of the hardships and dangers of the work, they submitted to orders without a complaint.

It was Meg who first developed a friendship with Canso, the Nova Scotian sailor shackled in the hold. Every mealtime, Mr. Pepper sent her with a plate of food down into the depths of the ship to feed the prisoner.

The first time she had gone below had been a frightening experience. She had come across the deck clutching onto a plate of gruel and a tin cupful of tea, hoping that nothing would spill. José opened the hatch for her and she slowly climbed down the wooden ladder into the pitch dark hold. As she stood on the cargo of squared timber, light from the open hatch streamed in on her and she squinted in an attempt to see into the dark recesses. The ship pitched through the waves, and she could hear the gurgling of the sea along the ship's hull and smell the foul odour of the bilge water.

"Where are you?" she asked with a quavering in her voice.

It seemed like a long time before she heard the rattle of the chain and a voice softly reply, "Over here."

The big man was shackled to a beam that supported the deck. The irons were firmly fastened to both wrists and ankles.

"Are you all right?" she asked anxiously.

Canso only grunted.

Without a word he wolfed down the watery gruel and washed down the hardtack with the bitter tea, but in handing back the plates the rough sailor looked up into Meg's face and smiled. A few hours later, when Meg came with his noon meal, Canso was more sociable, and at supper he even asked her a few questions about the running of the ship. The next day he insisted that she tell him exactly what she had seen or heard, and after he finished his meal he leaned back against the hull and talked.

The words flowed out of him in a casual sing-song voice filled with the slang of sailors. "The sea was always part of my life," he explained. "My father was a fisherman who went out to the Grand Banks every season. I was eight years old when I first went with him. By the time I was fourteen I was already a seasoned sailor, and I signed on before the mast in a Nova Scotian ship headed for San Francisco. For over ten years now the fo'c's'le's been my home. I've sailed under most flags in every type of deep-water ship and I've been in most ports from Africa to Australia and China to Canada."

Meg was fascinated with the sailor and looked forward to their meetings. On the evening of the second day, she persuaded John to come down into the hold with her.

It was a strange night. The wind out of the south-east was stronger now, creating heavy seas that peaked into white foam. The ship pitched up into the waves and then heaved down into the troughs making the masts shudder with the force of the impact. Dark storm clouds threatened to bring showers at any moment.

Meg got the prisoner his meal. The two of them went on deck. John opened the hatchway and they disappeared below. Once in the hold, the boy stood at the bottom of the ladder waiting for his eyes to adjust to the murky light. "Over here, John," he heard his sister whisper. Inching his way through the darkness, he held his arms out in front to keep his balance against the violently rolling ship. Then he settled down on the squared timber cargo beside Meg and leaned up against the curved hull.

Canso ate his meal of gruel and potatoes in silence. With each movement the seaman's chains rattled. After he finished he leaned back against the hull beside them.

"Feels like a strong blow up above," he commented. "These are treacherous waters. Many a ship's been driven ashore on Anticosti Island or the Gaspé coast."

"Is it dangerous?" asked Meg.

"It's always dangerous in any ship. The best place to be in a storm is as far away from land as possible. Then you're not in danger of being driven up on a shore and pounded to pieces on the rocks. But then with an old ship like this, being in deep water wouldn't even help much."

"What do you mean?" asked John.

"She's old. Eighteen, maybe twenty years old. She was built up some Nova Scotian creek and was as solid a craft as you could find anywhere in the world, but she's logged many miles since then. Now she's getting tender and there's not many voyages left in her."

"You mean the ship's unsafe?" asked Meg.

Canso was silent for a moment, listening to the movement of the big windjammer. "Hear that bilge water sloshing about in the bottom of the hold? The crew has been working the pumps on the two dog watches and there's still a lot of water in that hold. The hull is tender, the ship's timbers are old and soft and the sea soaks through them like they were paper."

The three of them sat in the semidarkness listening to the bilge and the rushing of the water on the other side of the hull. The *Scotian* seemed to be heaving more violently now because the sea was running high, and the timbers creaked and moaned with the motion.

Canso began again, "Any sailor who's ever set foot on a deck would know there's trouble aboard this ship. Look at it. The cap'n didn't have a pilot take us down river and there was no tug to tow us into the channel. Maybe Cap'n Barnard knows the river well, but any seaman will tell you he's taking a chance with this ship. It can only mean that he's saving money, and that's not a good sign for the beginning of an outward-bound voyage. Think of other things. There's no second mate aboard. On a big three-masted ship like this there is usually a mate for each watch, letting the cap'n stay free. But on the *Scotian* the cap'n's looking after the first watch himself. Then there's no carpenter and no sailmaker and the cap'n's cut down his crew to its bare bones. How many hands are there, lad?"

John thought for a moment. "There's nine. Ten if you want to count me, but I'm only kitchen help."

"Ten altogether, and this on a nine-hundred-and-sixty-ton craft. That's barely enough sailors to run a coastal schooner."

"It's terrible what they do to sailors," said Meg. "Who'd want to go to sea anyway?"

Canso laughed softly. "Aye, it's not much of a life. The loneliness is the worst. A sailor usually has no wife, no children, no money, no future. But then there's the freedom. You can visit different ports — see different people. When you learn to sail you do something worthwhile — you achieve something."

"I ... I'd like to learn," John said quietly. "But the captain won't give me a chance."

Canso sighed. "It's bad to start out on a ship like the *Scotian*. The officers drive us, and we're wanted for our labour and nothing else. That's how they look at us. We aren't to think. The first little complaint we make and we're clapped in irons, or rope-ended or something worse. The officers treat a crew like brutes and we act like brutes. There's nothing that we can do."

"It's not fair!" said Meg angrily.

"That may be, but you're not about to change it on this voyage."

"And why not? We should go to the cap'n and demand that he release you and treat the crew better."

"We can't do that, Meg," said her brother, annoyed.

"Why not? Who is this Cap'n Barnard? Look at what he's done to us and to Canso here."

"But he's the captain," said John.

"It's not right, is it, Canso? You tell him."

It was a moment before the sailor replied. "I tell you that this voyage will be no pleasure cruise. We're aboard this ship and there's little we can do about it."

They lapsed into silence. The hold was gloomy, cold and damp. The pitch and heave of the ship through the rough seas tossed them back and forth. They could hear the water rushing past the hull and the bilge sloshing below them. Occasionally there was the scurry of rats close by. As they sat, rain began pattering on the deck above them, and they could hear the whistling of the strong wind through the rigging.

Suddenly there was a darkened form in the open hatchway as a man laboriously made his way down the ladder. It was Mr. Ryerson, the bosun. He was a short, stocky man with powerful arms, but he was old — well past sixty — and iron-grey hair flowed out under his cap. He steadied himself with one hand on the ladder and peered into the darkness.

"Where are you, Canso?" he said in a Nova Scotian accent.

As the sailor sat up, the irons rattled. "Over here."

The bosun made his way in the direction of the sound, his eyes still adjusting to the dim light. The ship pitched and he stumbled. When he made it to where they were sitting he was surprised to find Meg and John. "What are you two doing here?"

"We brought Canso his supper," replied Meg.

"Well, you shouldn't linger to talk to a man in irons. He's under charge and the cap'n wouldn't like it."

"Why did he put Canso in irons?" asked Meg sharply. "It's not fair."

The bosun was surprised at this defiance. "Are you questioning the cap'n's authority?"

"It's not fair. And it's not fair that he shanghaied John and me and the rest of the crew."

"Your brother signed on fair and square. I saw the papers myself, and you're a stowaway."

"But the crimp forced him to sign the paper. Isn't that right, John?"

John reluctantly was drawn into the argument. "Yes, it's true."

"I can't believe that. The cap'n has to get his crew, but he wouldn't force anyone against his will."

"Well I believe them," added Canso. "The crimp drugged me and the next thing I knew I was aboard ship headed for the open sea."

"The cap'n couldn't do that."

Canso was getting angry. "Look for yourself, bosun. He was desperate to get a crew and he'd do anything for it."

"I'll not have you talking against the captain like this," said the bosun angrily. "I've sailed with him for many a year and I've never seen him hard on his sailors. I remember him as a boy younger than this lad, when he was learnin' on the foredeck. He felt the hardships like every sailor and he's always remembered it. Now he has his own ship for the first time. He bought it. Put his own life savings into it and borrowed heavily. He's not going to change, now that he's the master."

"But the ship's tender, bos'n," said Canso. "And he's sailing short-handed. You know that better than most. He's into trouble, and if I know things, it'll be taken out on the crew."

"I won't have you saying that!" The bosun shouted as if Canso had touched on a sore point. "This ship's as solid as any I've ever sailed on."

"But bos'n that's not true!"

"It is true! The master's as good a man as any that's held command, and there'll be no rumour coming from the fo'c's'le, Mr. Canso, or you'll be hearing from me!"

The bosun paused to collect himself. The others could only make out the outline of the stocky man bracing himself against the motion of the ship in the dim, gloomy light. When he began again there was a softness to his voice. "Try to understand.This is the first ship the cap'n can call his own — he has his whole life's savings tied up in it. He must get his cargo through or risk all that he has ever had."

"I don't care," said Meg, her quick temper getting the better of her. "The cap'n's an awful man to do this to us. He deserves the worst."

"No Meg, that's not true," said John. "He has his ship to worry about."

"He's a brute, John. Look at what he's done to us! What about our family? What about ourselves?"

"But Meg ...."

"Enough of this!" shouted the bosun. "I'll not have a person aboard ship talking against the master, and that even goes for you, missy!" The bosun was quiet as if the argument had drained him of energy. When he began again his voice was under control. "The cap'n sent me below to release you, Canso. Heavy seas are running and these are treacherous waters. The barometer has dropped almost out of sight. We'll need every hand to sail this ship tonight."

Before the bosun had finished unshackling the sailor they heard the captain shout a command from on deck. "All hands stow topsails! All hands stow topsails!"

Canso stood up rubbing his wrists where they had been chafed by the irons. "Come on, John. They want all hands."

"But the captain ordered me below."

"Didn't you want to be a sailor?"

"Yes …."

"Come on! It's a bad storm and they'll need every hand to stow the sails. I'll show you how to do it." Canso began scrambling up the ladder and John followed him, uncertain of himself but not wanting to be left behind.

Meg was with the bosun. "What about me?" she shouted, but already the seamen were on deck.

CHAPTER 4

THE three-masted ship was lashed by the violence of the storm. Huge waves that rose steeply from trough to crest tossed the vessel about and the torrent of rain made the decks awash with water. There were still two hours of sunlight, but already the sky was dark and eerie. The wind howling through the rigging seemed in danger of blowing away every piece of canvas, along with some of the yards and masts.

The sailors rushed out of the forecastle on the double, dressed in their black oilskins and southwester hats. In a moment, they were into the shrouds and scrambling for the topsail.

Canso barely paused. "Come on John!" he shouted. "Let's get our oilskins!" He headed for the forecastle on the run with the boy at his heels.

Suddenly the captain was in their path, his arms held up for them to stop. "Up into that rigging!" he shouted. "You don't have time for oilskins."

Canso paused, bracing himself against the pitch of the ship. "We need them, cap'n! We'll get soaked and freeze up there."

"Into those shrouds! And I'll have no insubordination!" Canso angrily turned to the boy. "Here's your honourable captain," he said.

"You'll do as I say or you'll be in irons the rest of this voyage."

It seemed like the big sailor would continue the argument, but John pulled at his arm. "Come on, Canso! Come on!" he pleaded.

A moment later the two of them were climbing up the starboard mainmast shrouds. For John, the terror of being aloft was even more vivid this time. The masts swayed violently back and forth with each wave, and the higher he climbed, the greater the motion. The wind shrieked through the rigging and tugged at his clothes, stinging his eyes. Chilled and soaked to the skin, he climbed on, knowing that Canso was there to help him and determined that this time he would do his share of the work and take his share of the danger.

By the time he joined the sailors, they had stowed the royal sail and were taking in the topgallant sail. Canso motioned that he was going to move out onto the larboard side of the yard and that John was to follow him. Carefully, the boy fit his feet into the stirrups and edged his way out, his arm looped over the yard for support. The rigging swayed violently with the pitch of the ship, the rain lashed at his face, and the wind tore at his clothes with a fury. Canso was motioning the boy to pull up on the sail. The heavy canvas was already closely reefed, but it still strained against the wind and was hard to grasp. John's fingers got a hold and he began pulling with all of his strength. With a heave from all of the sailors, the heavy sail furled up, and, as the air spilled out of its pocket, it became easier to manage.

The sailors wrapped it securely on the yardarm and tied it into place.

A moment later they were scrambling down to the yard immediately below them. It took even greater effort, but it was not long before they had stowed the upper topsail. Then the crew went back to the mizzenmast at the aft of the ship. In his effort to stick beside Canso, John seemed to forget the dangers, and once among the sails he knew what to do. In spite of the driving wind and rain and the rolling of the ship, it was not more than a few minutes before the crew had stowed all of the topsails.

What remained on the windjammer were the lower topsails and the mainsails on the foremast and mainmast, the schooner sail on the mizzenmast and the three jibs. Now that some of the canvas had been stowed, the ship rode more easily through the heavy seas. Their task over, the crew made their way across the wet, slippery deck and disappeared into the forecastle.

John and Canso were soaked to the skin and they shivered in the cold damp room as they changed clothes. Canso was so angry he could not contain himself.

"Damn his soul!" he shouted to anyone listening. "Our cap'n doesn't even try to look after his sailors. Look at us! Soaked to the bone!"

"Stop it, Canso!" It was the bosun standing in the dim light of the doorway. "I've had enough of yer talkin' of the cap'n like that."

As Canso turned he gripped the side of a bunk with one of his huge hands. "This ship's a floating hell, bosun. With a madman as its cap'n!" he shouted angrily.

"Enough!" The bosun waited until Canso and the other sailors had settled. "The cap'n sent me to tell you that things could get worse. The barometer is still falling and the storm is stronger than ever. You may be wanted before the night is out, so sleep with your oilskins on."

Meg had come to the forecastle and she sat with John on his bunk listening to the talk around them. There was a feeling of resentment among the sailors and Canso's anger added a bitter element to it.

"This old tub's a tomb," said Tommy, one of the young Englishmen.

"Aye," said Hans, the burly Dutch sailor. "She's a wreck. We'll be down before the night's out."

"And she's shipping water badly," added Canso.

The crew members sat at the edge of their bunks waiting and listening to the storm and the talk around them. The two Portuguese sailors, Piedro and Santana, spoke to each other quietly in their own language. Georges and Joseph propped themselves up against the beams of the ship, waiting nervously for the next order. Scobie, a frightened, timid man, crouched on the bunk beside his friend Tommy, his eyes flashing from person to person as if expecting disaster at any moment.

"The captain's a madman," said Canso angrily. "The ship's so tender she's about to fall apart. Look at him. He stands there by the helmsman like he's on a death watch!"

Meg and John sat together, watching the shadowy forms in the darkened forecastle and talking in hushed voices. They were frightened. The ship pounded back and forth with the waves and moaned with every movement as if she was about to break up. All they could do was hold onto each other for support and hope they would survive.

It was not long before new orders were shouted. "All hands stow mainsails! All hands stow mainsails!"

The sailors scrambled up the ladder to the deck. The storm was worse now. It was almost dark, but they could see the outline of gigantic waves heaving and falling. The wind was strong, lashing the rain into their faces, and straining the canvas to the point where it seemed as if a sudden gust could bring the masts down.

This time it took the whole crew to work on each sail. They began at the forward mast by taking in the enormous lower topsail, and then moved onto the mainsail. After they were finished, they began work on the mainmast.

The new oilskins made John feel awkward and the job took every last ounce of his strength, but he had learned a new confidence in being aloft. The wind blew so loudly that he could not hear the orders, so he stuck close behind Canso and followed what he was doing.

John and Canso were on the larboard side of the mast working on the huge mainsail when the sailor, releasing it from its stays, suddenly had the rope dragged out of his grip. In a moment, the enormous sail cracked against the mast, almost sending the sailors pitching onto the deck, and splitting the sail as though it were made of tissue paper. The long strips of canvas snapped back and forth in the wind.

Canso took command. Leaning over the yard he grabbed a big part of the flapping sail in his arms, gave an enormous pull and furled it around the yardarm. But at the end of the yard, a piece of canvas still cracked violently in the wind.

"Get it, John!" Canso shouted, and he waved at the boy to gather in the canvas strip.

John inched his way along the footropes, holding grimly onto the yard and handrope. The further out he went the more the ship seemed to toss back and forth, until he feared that the end of the yard would dip into the crest of one of the huge waves and sweep him from his perch. But finally he was near the end; he curled his body over the yard, reached out into space with his one free arm, and grabbed the flapping canvas. The rough material cracked above his head, but he was able to get a handhold and pull it toward himself. Then he reached out again and again until he had the strip of canvas furled around the yard and tied into place. As he made his way back to the mast, John could see Canso smiling at him, and he knew that he had passed one of the tests of a seaman.

Without pausing to consider the damage or the risks, the crew moved back to the mizzenmast and lowered the huge fore-and-aft-rigged mizzen sail. Three of the sailors went forward and stowed all but one of the jibs. The captain needed it to keep the ship's head into the wind. When they had finished, the crew hurried back into the comparative comfort of the forecastle leaving the captain and José, who was doing his turn at the helm, to tend to the ship.

The storm pitched the vessel back and forth violently. The rain pounded on the deck heavily and the fierce wind howled through the rigging. Everyone knew that the ship was helpless before the storm. They were adrift in the St. Lawrence estuary with no power and no way of knowing their exact position. In the blackness of the night, a shore could be upon them before the captain could shout an order. Only good fortune could save them now.

The men sat on their bunks talking in low voices. The candle lantern flickered dimly, giving a grim appearance to their faces. As the minutes passed, the ship seemed to lurch even more violently through the heavy seas.

Suddenly the first mate was at the forecastle door. "All hands aft! All hands aft!"

The sailors scrambled onto the deck again wearing their oilskins and southwesters. It was almost black, but John could see enormous waves on both sides. The ship tossed up into a crest and then pounded down into the trough. Sheets of rain drove at them and the howling wind turned the surface of the sea into a mass of boiling foam. The deck was awash with water that poured off through the scuppers and back into the sea. As the crew made their way aft, they had to crouch almost double into the wind and inch their way along by holding onto the lifeline that was strung along the rail.

The ship had been pooped by a giant wave that had come rolling in over the man at the wheel. It splashed forward with great force, extinguishing the binnacle lamp and smashing in the cabin skylights at the rear of the ship. In spite of the difficult conditions, it was no more than a few minutes before the crew had spread boards over the skylight to keep out the water and had begun to swab out the ankle-deep water that sloshed about on the floor of the cabins.

Captain Barnard had not moved from his position beside the wheel. The helmsman had been terrified after the big wave had swamped them and the ship had begun skidding uncontrollably through the waves. The captain swore and shouted directions, but still they seemed to flounder out of control.

Canso and John were on deck. "We've got to control the ship or we'll go under!" one seaman shouted to the captain above the storm.

"The helmsman can't hold her!" The captain seemed desperate. Worry and fatigue lined his face.

For a moment the two men stared at each other, trying to size up the situation. There was much hatred and bitterness between them, but Canso could not stand by while the ship floundered. "I'll take the wheel!" he shouted.

Within moments he had lashed himself to the binnacle and grasped the spokes of the wheel in his giant hands. He was planted as firmly as a tree, his feet apart, using every ounce of strength to control the ship.

The wind was generally out of the east, but often gusts caught the rigging from all points of the compass. In an instant the ship could be whirled around by as much as ninety degrees and then it would be taking waves over the beam or the poop rail. Once Canso took over, he struggled to keep the bow into the waves by swinging the rudder back and forth to catch the current and the wind. It took every ounce of his concentration, but the old wooden ship reacted as if it had become a part of him.

Once they had finished cleaning the after-cabins, all of the crew made their way to the forecastle, leaving Canso and the captain to fight the storm alone. John and Meg, huddling in the crew's quarters, found the morale of the sailors very low. As time dragged on, no one spoke and no one slept; they waited on their bunks in the flickering lantern light, ready to make a rush for the boats the moment they heard the hull splintering. Minutes went by like hours and hours seemed to be days, as the wind screeched outside and the ship pitched and creaked in the turbulent sea.

Toward dawn Meg whispered to her brother that they would have to go aft to help Mr. Pepper. Outside, the storm was at its height. The wind was so strong that it blew off the tops of the waves before they had time to rise, and as far as the eye could see, flying foam covered the water. John and Meg could see the two men standing by the wheel at the stern in the dim light, fighting to control the ship.

Mr. Pepper had prepared a pot of tea and when they got to the galley, he sent the two of them above deck with a cup for each of the men on duty.

Canso smiled broadly when he saw them and gratefully drank his tea in two gulps. The captain looked grim. His face sagged with fatigue, and he seemed to hold himself upright only with an iron will. Once he had finished his tea, he untied himself and disappeared into his cabin. A moment later he was back on deck with navigation instruments.

He crouched over so John could hear. "Tie yourself in, boy, and search off the starboard beam for land."

"Aye, sir," John replied. "And you. Get below and help Mr. Pepper," he said to Meg.

"I want to stay above deck!"

"Get below now!" the captain shouted threateningly.

Meg wanted very much to be with the others, but she could not openly defy the captain. Reluctantly, she bent into the wind and headed back to the galley. John had tied himself in and searched off the starboard beam, but the rain and the heavy weather had closed the visibility to less than a mile.

The captain's calculations took some time. He cautiously returned to the deck twice to take new sightings of the sun with his sextant and returned below deck for his calculations. Finally he was satisfied and returned holding a chart under his oilskins to protect it from the elements.

The three of them huddled around. "I figure we're about forty-nine degrees, twenty-five minutes north latitude, which is about here." He pointed to a spot on the chart with his blunt finger. "I couldn't get a longitude reading and I don't know how far we are off the Gaspé coast, but I'd estimate we've been driven back down the estuary about fifty miles."

Canso nodded thoughtfully. "The wind is coming directly out of the north now. It'll drive us back onto the coast and there's nothing we can do unless we can get a sail on her," he shouted.

"I know." The captain's voice showed his worry.

"We'll have to set an east-northeast course. That'll take us out into the Gulf."

"But Canso, it may take the masts right out of her. She's an old ship."

"We've got to try, Cap'n. Otherwise it'll just be a matter of time and we'll be pounded to pieces on the shore."

The captain, bending almost double into the wind, made his way forward. Canso and John could see him shouting down into the forecastle and within moments all hands were scrambling out onto the deck. They made their way back over the pitching deck to the poop, loosened the rope leading to the yard of the main mizzen sail and all of the men began pulling on it. The sail went up with a terrible roar as it flapped violently in the wind. Then it was tied into place.

Four hands were sent forward to rig the rest of the jibs. They inched their way into the footropes, holding on tightly to the jib boom as the bow pitched into the waves, sending showers of sea water over them. Within moments the three jibs were unfurled and flapping in the wind.

Canso waited at the wheel until all hands had a firm grip and then slowly began turning the wheel to starboard. The big ship began swinging. The huge mizzen sail cracked across as it caught the wind, straining the canvas and rigging. But it held. The ship dipped over on the starboard beam until it seemed as if the rail was going to go under the water.

Almost immediately the ship picked up some momentum and began slicing diagonally through the waves. It was a new and frightening roll as she skidded down into the troughs of the waves and then went back on the other beam as she climbed the next wave. But in spite of the violent sway and the creaking of her timbers, the old ship held firm.

On the captain's orders, John went back to the poop deck and tied himself to the starboard rail to act as lookout. A new sense of hope and optimism was shared by the crew and the boy felt more relaxed.

As he studied the seething water, Captain Barnard suddenly bent over him. The captain's exhaustion made his eyes sunken and bloodshot, but a brief smile played over his lips. "You may be a seaman yet, boy," he said gently. He rested his hand on John's shoulder for a brief moment and then turned away and walked back toward the helmsman.

CHAPTER 5

IT'S just not fair, John, that's all," Meg was saying. "You have fun climbing through the rigging and I have to work all day in the galley with Mr. Pepper."

It was the day after the big storm had blown itself out and already the heavy clouds were breaking up. They were travelling east-southeast before a stiff breeze through the Gulf of St. Lawrence.

John and Meg were on the foredeck arguing. "But Meg, you can't go up into the rigging. The captain has strictly forbidden it."

"I just want to try it out, that's all. I've got on sailors' clothes and light shoes."

"You can't Meg."

"Well, I don't care. Why don't you go back and work with Mr. Pepper in that stinking old kitchen? I want to have some fun too."

"You know the cap'n won't let you, because you're a girl."

"I can work just as hard as you John Bains, and don't tell me any different!"

"But Meg, the captain …." John was exasperated.

"It doesn't matter what he thinks. I'm going up into the rigging and that's all there is to it. You can go and help the cook."

"No Meg, don't be silly!"

"I'm going!" She started heading for the shrouds of the foremast.

"Meg!" But John's pleas fell on deaf ears. His sister pulled herself up on the rail and nimbly started climbing toward the main yard.

"What's going on here?" It was Mr. Ryerson, the bosun. He could not believe that a young girl like Meg could be going up into the shrouds. "What are you doing?"

John gestured hopelessly. "She wants to go climbing in the rigging."

"She can't do that!"

"It's not fair, Mr. Ryerson," Meg shouted from the shrouds. "John gets to have all the fun and I have to stay in the galley with Mr. Pepper."

"But you can't be a sailor, Meg. It's unheard-of for girls."

"Well I'll show you what I can do," she said, and climbed a little higher into the shrouds.

A number of sailors who were on the watch stopped working and gathered around. "You tell him, Meg!" shouted Tommy. "Climb up till you feel the wind," added José.

"Come down at once!" the bosun said crossly. He seemed uncertain how to react. If he was to follow Meg into the shrouds, he could easily be left behind and become the laughing stock of the crew, but if he ignored her, then it would seem as if the officers could not impose discipline.

Meg was equally unsure of herself. She did not want to appear unruly and disrespectful of Mr. Ryerson, but she wanted to make the point that she was capable of working aloft. "I won't come down!" she shouted. "Not until you let me have a turn working in the rigging like my brother."

"The cap'n won't let you do that, Meg."

"What's going on here?" It was the mate, Mr. Mckenzie.

"Meg Bains is up in the rigging and won't come down," explained the bosun. "She says some fool thing about wanting to learn to be a sailor like her brother."

"Come down at once!" ordered the mate.

"Stay up there!" shouted Tommy good-humouredly. "Climb to the royals!" added Georges. The other crew members shouted their agreement. They loved the spectacle of this young girl defying the ship's officers.

Meg entered into the spirit of things. "Come and catch me!" she shouted, and set off scrambling up the shrouds as fast as she could go.

Mr. Mckenzie was known as a good seaman and he was not about to ignore this challenge from a girl, especially with the whole crew looking on. With a laugh, he sprang into the shrouds and began scrambling after her.

"Climb Meg, climb!" someone shouted. "Come on girl! You can beat him!" All of the crew were shouting and making bets as if it was a race. They were delighted that Meg was so full of spirit. Even the bosun was caught up in the excitement and cheered her on.

Meg climbed as fast as she could, but the mate came at twice her speed. They were both laughing and breathless with the excitement of the chase.

The captain was suddenly on deck. "What's going on here?" He was standing outside the circle of sailors. The set of his chin and the hard look of his eyes showed that he was not amused. The shouting of the sailors stopped immediately. Meg and the mate froze in mid-motion.

"What is this, Mr. Mckenzie?"

The mate tried awkwardly to explain. "I … I …." A moment later he was on the deck and Meg was soon beside him.

"Yes, Mr. Mckenzie. What is the explanation?" The captain's stern face showed not a trace of emotion.

"It was Meg. She … she was in the rigging. It was just a game, Cap'n."

"A game, Mr. Mckenzie? A game?!"

"Yes sir. You see I …."

"It was my fault, sir," Meg interrupted. "I wanted to go aloft and Mr. Mckenzie was trying to get me down."

The captain searched the faces of the sailors, and then examined the bosun and mate before looking back at Meg. "I want everyone here to know that no girl is to be aloft on this ship. Do you understand?"

"But captain, why can't I learn to be a sailor? It's not fair."

"Your job is to be steward. You're to help Mr. Pepper and nothing else."

"Well I don't think that's right," said Meg, stamping her foot angrily and folding her arms across her chest. "I think I should be given a chance."

"That's enough, missy," replied the captain angrily. "If I catch you up in the rigging again, there'll be discipline meted out. Do you understand?"

"Yes sir," Meg finally said, resigned to her defeat.

"Now you sailors get back to work and there'll be no more of this foolishness. Move, on the double!"

The crew members hurried away, but before they were out of earshot they could hear the captain begin to give a dressing-down to the young mate. "Mr. Mckenzie, there is no excuse for this behavior. You should never play games with the crew …."

The crew went back to work with bitter feelings toward the captain. Many had felt the sharpness of his tongue in the few days since they had been out of port: The general opinion was that he was a hard-driving master with little regard for his company. To witness a dressing-down of the mate for what was a bit of light-hearted fun only confirmed this opinion.

Since the storm, the crew had been labouring constantly to bring things into shape. The bosun had discovered four feet of water in the ship's well, and for three consecutive watches the crew had to man the pumps. They stood on the deck about midships and, with two men on each end of a long-handled rocker pump, they worked the bar back and forth monotonously.

John was on the mate's watch, and in the morning he worked with Canso, Tommy and José. Santana took the first two hours at the helm and then switched places with José. Within half an hour John's shoulders and arms were aching from the effort, but he doggedly kept at the chore, knowing that if he were to give up, his mates would have to carry on alone.

The singing of various pumping shanties made the task easier. Tommy, the English sailor, led them in songs such as *Mr. Stormalong* and *Since Rovin's Been My Ru-Eye-In.* But after three hours of the work, the boy was exhausted. He got through the last hour of the watch only on sheer will. The captain had said he would be a sailor, and he was determined to prove himself.

The crew of the captain's watch continued their work without letup, and when the mate's watch came back on deck four hours later, they manned the pumps again. Everyone hated the work, and they grumbled constantly.

"She's leaking as if one of the timbers on the hull had come off her," said Tommy.

"The pumping, she will be the death of us," added José in his heavy Spanish accent.

Canso made no attempt to cover up his outrage at their predicament. "She shouldn't be shipping this much water," he said when the mate came by.

"The cap'n went down in the hold," said Mr. Mckenzie. "And he says she'll be fine."

"I say she must have sprung a big leak to still have water in her hold after eight hours of pumping."

"The cap'n says it's fine, Canso, and he knows better than any of us."

"Well, it's not fine." The big sailor was openly defiant.

"That'll be enough, Canso."

As the pumping resumed, the mate stood over the sailors for a long time, waiting to hear if there would be any more comments. Then he went back to the poop deck to check on the helmsman. As soon as he was out of earshot, the sailors resumed their complaining,

"An old tub. That's what she is. She'll go down before we ever hit a port," said Tommy under his breath.

Canso was furious. "I tell you this ship's not fit and that's the truth of it. The hull is so tender you could push your fist through it in places. The storm gave her such a battering that leaks have opened up. I swear to you that we'll pump all the way to Jamaica unless something's done about it."

"But what can we do, Canso?" asked John.

"The cap'n should take her up on some beach, roll her on her side and recaulk the whole hull. That's what ought to be done."

"Lot of chance for that," said José bitterly.

The four of them lapsed into silence. As they pumped, the swing of the big handles made a rhythmical thumping noise. Canso spoke again, "I tell you we've got to do something about it. Otherwise we may end up a hundred fathoms down."

"But we're only sailors," said John. "The captain knows best."

"What are you saying boy?"

"It's just that ... well ... we can't challenge the captain's decision."

"He'll have to listen to us," said Canso emphatically. "That's all there is to it." The discussion seemed to make the big seaman angry and the boy did not want to say any more to annoy him.

An hour after the watch had begun, the mate climbed into the hold and returned to say that the ship was almost dry. They stored the pump handle and then the bosun organized more work.

They all went below to the sail locker and helped drag out an enormous roll of canvas. It took the four crew members as well as the bosun and the mate to wrestle the heavy, awkward material up on deck. When it was spread out, it took almost the whole midships from one rail to the other.

There was no sailmaker aboard ship, but any of the officers and several of the able seamen were competent to cut a sail tailored to the needs of the ship. The bosun had spent most of the day making careful measurements of the mainsail that had been torn during the storm, and he measured the canvas with care, placing chalk marks on the outline and marking where each crinkle and reef band would be sewn. Then the two able seamen, Canso and Tommy, along with the bosun, each took big scissors and carefully cut the canvas on the lines.

Once the sail was cut, they started the difficult task of sewing it. On all four sides, ropes had to be sewn into the hems to give the edges strength. Reef bands had to be stitched into place and small loops called crinkles had to be sewn at the sail's edge so that various lines holding the sail into place could be attached. Sailmaking was an exacting task, but most of the sailors enjoyed it because it gave them a chance to sit on deck, working their needle and palm (the leather which protected their hand) in comparative comfort.

They had just begun the sewing of the sail when the bosun rang the bell indicating the end of the watch, and the mate's watch went below. They gathered in a small room near the galley in the after section of the ship which was the sailors' mess.

Within moments, Meg came out with their supper. It was duff, a type of dumpling made out of flour and water floating in a thin broth.

"What is this?" demanded Canso. "We're having duff already! We've barely left port." Duff was usually eaten only on long voyages after the provisions had run out.

The others were equally hostile. Santana curled back his lips in disgust. José was fuming, and he pushed away his plate.

"Is this something we're expected to eat?" Tommy asked Meg.

The young girl smiled. "The other watch wasn't happy with it either."

"We're hungry and need better than this."

"You'll have to ask the cook, Tommy."

"Mr. Pepper! Mr. Pepper!" the impulsive Englishman shouted. In a moment the cook poked his head into the room. He wore a white apron and on his head was his black bowler hat.

"Why have we got duff, Mr. Pepper?" Tommy demanded.

"If it's complaints that you've got about the food, then you'll have to see the cap'n," the cook said in his broad cockney accent. "'Tis he that bought the provisions."

"You mean there's nothing to eat other than duff?" Canso asked in disbelief.

"She's a long voyage to the Indies. If we eat everthin' that's good in the first week, then we'll have to live on duff and rotten tea for the last few weeks. I 'ave me orders."

"But why didn't he bring more food?" Canso asked.

Mr. Pepper glanced nervously at the others. "I'm not sure. All I hear is the rumours. It's just that — well — you must of 'eard. The cap'n's bankrupt they say. 'E 'as no money and the banks are demanding that 'e sells 'is ship. What with 'ard times 'e was lucky to get this cargo. 'E figures that if 'e can make some money 'e can pay off the bank in Halifax and the ship will be 'is."

"And so because of this he takes it out on his sailors," Canso burst out. "That's it, isn't it? He has no money to pay decent wages so he shanghais sailors. He cuts down on his officers and crew. He has no second mate, no sailmaker, no carpenter, and he's only got ten sailors where he should have at least fifteen. Now it turns out that we've got no food."

"We should mutiny for this!" said Tommy pounding the table.

"We've got to do something," added Canso.

Meg had been following the discussion closely. "That's right. We've got to stand up for ourselves."

"But what can we do?" asked John.

"We should demand that the captain take the ship into a port to be recaulked and get more provisions," said Canso. "We've got to do something or we may all go down with this leaky tub."

"The captain won't do that," said John.

"Then we'll have to force him. We'll demand it!"

"But that would be mutiny," added Santana.

Tommy was angry. "Damn the mutiny."

"What would the authorities do if we were found guilty?" asked John quietly.

Canso sighed and looked from one to the other. "Aye. We'd be hung. They show no mercy."

The sailors were silent for a long time. Slowly John picked up his spoon and took a taste of the duff. It was a gooey, sticky mass of flour but the boy's hunger forced him to take another bite. In time the others picked up their spoons and without a word the crew ate their duff.

In the next few days the *Scotian* sailed southeast through the Cabot Strait, between Newfoundland and Cape Breton Island. Then they altered course to south by southeast and once they were clear of Cape Breton, they changed again to south by southwest. They would sail about one hundred miles off the American Atlantic coast down to the West Indies.

A mood of defeat and resignation settled over the crew, and the joking and horseplay that were normal among sailors were absent on this voyage. The men complained often, and with reason. Every day the crew spent at least six hours at the pumps until the ship was dry. That was boring work hated by everyone, and the constant hard physical labour left them exhausted.

All of the equipment aboard ship was in very poor condition. The winches and standing rigging were beginning to rust badly and the sails were thin and frayed from wear. Once out of the North Atlantic, a squall sprung on them unexpectedly. Before they could stow all the canvas, the forward royal sail backed out against the mast and split. It was old and frayed, but rather than replace it, the bosun found some discarded canvas; the sailors fashioned a patch, and they rigged the sail up again.

The quality of food gradually worsened. The Boston beans ran out and soon the packages of dried prunes were all eaten. More and more frequently, Mr. Pepper was forced to serve the hungry sailors duff and hardtack, with beef hash and potatoes. Even the tea, which the sailors loved, got worse as the water in the big wooden barrels became brackish. Nothing aggravated the men's already shortened tempers more than their constant hunger.

But in spite of the conditions, young Meg Bains was the only one to rebel. She was trapped in her job and she longed for ways to escape. Often in the afternoon after her chores were finished, she went above deck to watch the sailors work. Both the captain and the mate wanted her to stay below. They would tell her that if she ran out of work, she was to come to them and they would find her more to do, but on no account was she to bother the sailors.

This irritated Meg. The last thing she wanted was to be trapped forever in the galley, and she was further annoyed at the thought that she was expected to work all the time. The way she viewed it, her brother John was having fun, while she was caught in drudgery.

It was not long before Meg decided to discard her long dress and wear seaman's gear of heavy canvas trousers and a woollen work shirt. After supper on the day she first wore the new outfit, the captain called her into his quarters. He sat behind the beautiful mahogany desk in his state room with his dark blue coat on, looking very stern. "Miss Bains," he began awkwardly. "What is the meaning of this outfit that you are wearing?" The captain was always very formal in his dealings with Meg.

In spite of her thirteen years, Meg would not be easily intimidated. "I find it more comfortable, Cap'n."

"Well, I want you to wear a dress."

"It's easier to work about a ship in sailors' clothes rather than a dress. And anyway, there's no one here to see me but the crew and they don't care."

The captain contained his anger with an effort. "I don't like it. I say you should wear a dress and look like a girl, not some rough sailor."

"That's silly, Cap'n. I want to be comfortable."

"I don't like this one bit, Miss Bains. I remind you that you're a stowaway on this voyage, and now you defy me."

Meg was uncertain of herself. "But Cap'n, I'm more comfortable this way."

"You'll do as I say. Now get changed."

She nodded and left the officers' mess, but she was far from satisfied.

That night, she saw John and told him what had happened. Her brother was horrified. "You'll have to change back into your dresses, Meg," he said.

"Why? He can't tell me what to wear." And with that she stomped back to her quarters even more determined than she had been before.

The next morning Meg got up, dressed in her sailor's gear and went to work. Mr. Pepper could see trouble brewing, but when he caught a hint of the stubbornness in the girl's eye he thought the better of saying anything.

When the captain had settled himself at the officers' table, Meg went in to serve him as if she had not a care in the world. The master stared at her in disbelief. Not only was she contravening his word, but she was doing it as if inviting disciplinary action.

"Miss Bains!" the captain said angrily. "I have told you time and again that you are to wear dresses!"

"I won't do it!" Meg slammed the tray she had been carrying down onto the table, stood up full size and shouted angrily at the master. "You can order me all you like, but if you won't let me work as a sailor, then at least I'm going to dress like one."

For a moment the captain seemed stunned at the girl's defiance, but suddenly he was laughing gently. "I give up. Do what you like."

Meg went back to the galley, a bit astonished at her easy victory, but nonetheless proud of herself. If the men aboard the *Scotian* were too cowardly to stand up to the captain, at least the girls in the crew had some temper and spirit.

CHAPTER 6

THE trip south was John's introduction into the life of a sailor. The boy had to learn, and learn fast, so that he could contribute his share to the running of the vessel. But this was no easy chore. A green hand had to do more than learn to work in the rigging. He had to memorize the names of all the sails, ropes and fittings so that he would know exactly where to put his hand the moment an order was given and what effect it would have on the running of the ship.

This was just the beginning. A good seaman automatically calculated the direction and velocity of the wind — whether it was steady or gusty — and the pitch and shape of the waves. He had to know how much strain the rigging of the ship could take in a gale and estimate the weight of the cargo or ballast to judge the ship's stability. And during a calm he had to know exactly at what angle to set the sail to catch the least breath of wind.

John's physical strength and natural ability made him an excellent student. The first thing the boy conquered was his fear of being aloft. Even on calm days the topmost yards swayed back and forth with each pitch of the waves, but when the seas were running high, the masts were whipped with such force that it took every bit of strength just to hold on. Mr. Mckenzie believed in a very direct education. He ordered the boy aloft as often as he could so that John could practise scrambling up the shrouds and inching his way precariously out toward the yardarms. With this constant training it was not long before the boy was running through the rigging with as much speed as the best sailor aboard ship.

All the members of the mate's watch contributed to John's apprenticeship. Often Mr. Mckenzie came aloft to show him different parts of the rigging and explain how each contributed to the running of the ship. Santana loved to climb the rigging, and he frequently would go up with John to perform chores. Canso was always at the boy's shoulder giving explanations of how the sails were trimmed, and he, along with Tommy, patiently showed the boy how to cut and sew the canvas. José taught him a number of useful sailors' knots and showed him how rope and cable were spliced. All the sailors aboard the *Scotian* followed their trade with pride and a serious dedication which they were anxious to share with anyone eager to listen.

John learned very quickly. By the second week out in the Atlantic the mate had enough confidence in the boy to give him a regular turn at the helm — two hours out of twenty-four. This was the best time of all for John. To stand on the poop deck of the big ship with the huge spoked wheel in his hands, feeling the waves tug at the rudder and the wind in the sails, made it seem as if he was in possession of the whole ship. Like the other sailors, John was beginning to have a love for the *Scotian* and a respect for the sea and wind.

They were on one of the most frequently travelled routes of the Nova Scotian windjammers. The ships carried timber or salt cod south from any one of a dozen Canadian or Newfoundland ports and came back loaded with sugar, rum or salt. Frequently, they followed a triangular route: south with cod or timber, across to Europe with sugar or rum, and back to Canada with their holds filled with manufactured goods or emigrants.

As the ship headed south, the weather became hotter with each passing day. Often they sailed with brisk westerly winds off the starboard beam on a sea of long rolling swells. Sometimes they ran into storms that would buffet them about for a day or two, but more often in late summer they were plagued with calms. Then the sails would hang limp without a breath of air in them and every person aboard the *Scotian* sweltered above and below decks.

Occasionally they would see the white sails of another ship and they would run up the red ensign and try to identify the type of rigging and the ship's nationality. Once, a hundred miles off Cape Cod, a steam-driven emigrant ship passed so close to them that they could see the faces of the people crowded onto the decks. But except for these rare sightings, they were alone in the vast ocean.

In spite of the calm of the sea the captain drove his crew incessantly. He sailed the *Scotian* as if she were a clipper on a fast passage rather than a creaky, aged wooden ship. When a gale was blowing, he would leave the canvas on as long as possible in order to get every bit of speed out of the wind. Only at the last moment would he give the order to reef the sails, and it would be a fierce storm before he would stow one of them. Even when there was a calm he would pace the deck, studying the wind and ordering the sailors aloft to adjust the sails.

It was the pumping that they hated most of all. For six hours a day, two hours on and two hours off, they manned the pumps in the blistering heat. It was back-breaking, monotonous work that left their muscles aching and their bodies burned black from the hot tropical sun. The work went on without a letup, hour upon hour, until the ship's hold was dry.

After three weeks John had grown hardened to shipboard life. His arms and shoulders had developed new strength from climbing in the riggings; his hands were calloused from handling the pump and ropes; his skin was burned a dark brown and his hair was bleached almost white, but still he found the physical work in the hot sun exhausting.

One afternoon in the height of a heatwave, John and Canso were roped into ladders and lowered over the side of the ship to scrape and paint the hull. There was not a breath of wind. The sun beat down from overhead and its blinding reflection from the water made the temperature soar. They worked without relief, scraping and scrubbing the hull with every ounce of energy in their bodies. Finally John began to feel lightheaded. He paused to rest, his hand wiping his brow. His eyes would not focus, and he seemed dizzy.

"Canso … Canso, I feel sick. I …." His eyes were glassy and his knees started to buckle. The scraper he had been using slipped out of his hand and fell into the sea.

"Canso …." He almost lost consciousness.

Quick as a cat the big sailor freed himself from the ropes and leaned over to support the boy. "Help! Give us a hand!" he shouted. "It's John!"

In a moment Santana was down the ladder and Georges was leaning over the rail to grasp an arm. Between the three of them they freed the boy from his ropes and lifted him up onto the deck. A moment later José came running with a cup of water.

John was delirious. "I lost the scraper, Canso. It went into the sea."

"That's all right, boy. Don't think of it. You need to get out of this sun." The big seaman had picked him up in his arms and was carrying him to rest in the shade of the foredeck.

Suddenly Captain Barnard was there. "What's wrong with that boy?"

"He passed out with the heat, Cap'n," replied Canso. "He needs rest."

"He passed out with the heat, you say? Any sailor who does that aboard my ship will not have an easy time of it. Put him down, Canso. I'll look after him. Now you men get back to work."

"But Cap'n …." Canso tried to protest.

"You heard me. Back to work!" Slowly the men retreated, leaving the master standing over the half-conscious boy. A few minutes later John had rejoined his mates. The captain had swabbed his face with water, and when he was feeling better sent him back to work again.

"That man has no feeling," Canso murmured to the boy as they worked, but the seaman was unwilling to challenge the captain's authority.

As the trip continued Canso spent more and more of his time with John and Meg. In spite of his open friendliness and good humour he seemed a lonely man who was trying to find something of his own past. Often he would encourage them to talk about their family in Ottawa and life in the lumber shanties. He shared stories with them about his childhood in a Nova Scotian fishing village.

Often during those hot afternoons John and Canso spent their off-duty time fishing. The two of them would get fishing lines, hooks and bait and climb up into the jib-boom shrouds at the bow of the ship. It was wonderful to be alone in the riggings, feeling the warm tropical sun on their shoulders and the motion of the big windjammer as it sliced through the seas. They would laze in the sun talking and telling stories until they almost forgot what they were doing. Then, suddenly one of them would get a strike. The line would go taut and yank them hard enough to be pulled from their perch. The other would tie his line off, get the grappling hook, and join in the intense struggle to get the dolphin or sailfish aboard.

On the days when they made a good catch, all the crew would gather around to admire the prize, and then Mr. Pepper would carefully cut enough fillets for everyone.

At least for a couple of days the crew would have welcome relief from the monotonous shipboard diet of salt pork, bread and hardtack.

With the heat wave the crew spent much of their time on deck to avoid the oppressive conditions of the forecastle. At night, once the sun was set, the only sailors on duty would be the helmsman, the lookout and one of the officers. In the early evening the others would lounge on the foredeck smoking their clay pipes, telling stories and singing songs.

One evening Meg and Mr. Pepper came out of the galley to enjoy the cool evening air just as the sun was setting into a beautiful golden sky. Meg sat down with John and Canso, and the three chatted quietly until Tommy brought out his squeeze box and began playing a tune. First he started with a chord and then broke into a lively piece adapted from a sailor's song but sounding a good deal like a North England jig. Tommy's music was wild and it seemed to go faster and faster with the playing.

In a moment Scobie was on his feet dancing the hornpipe and then he was joined by Mr. Pepper, complete with bowler hat and heavy shoes. Soon Georges was with them, his canvas pants turned up and his bare feet slapping the rhythm of the music on the deck. Mr. Pepper gave a wild performance, raising his knees up to his chin and stamping the deck with his heels: Constantly he had to catch his bowler hat and pull it back on his forehead so the others would not see his bald patch. Scobie danced in the style of an Irish jig, with short leg movements and his arms held stiffly by his side, while Georges used Greek arm movements and knee bends. As the music got faster, more of the sailors joined in. Santana and Piedro showed off a Portuguese folk dance, and José swayed his whole body in a Caribbean rhumba. The last to get to his feet was Canso, and, in spite of his size, he danced gracefully with a step much like that of the Scottish highland fling.

The foredeck pounded with the rhythm of the dancing feet as Tommy's music increased its tempo. The sweat poured off the faces of the sailors, soaking their shirts, but the men danced furiously to keep up with the beat. On and on Tommy played, faster and faster the music went, until the seamen were whirling and bouncing with the effort. Then finally with a flourish it was over.

After a second tune, the pace of Tommy's music slowed and he began to play seamen's shanties. He led them in a tune called *Mr. Stormalong*, and then Mr. Pepper sang the verses to *Donkey Riding*. Finally, after a lot of urging, Canso agreed to sing the Nova Scotian song. It was a ballad telling the story of a Nova Scotian sailor who was sad because he would be separated from those he loved when he went to sea. When it came to the chorus Canso's voice broke with emotion.

So farewell to Nova Scotia, the sea bound coast!
Let your mountains dark and dreary be,
For when I am far away on the briny ocean tossed
Will you ever heave a sigh and a wish for me?

With the last refrain the words trailed off across the water leaving the seamen with thoughts of their own homeland. Canso silently got to his feet to look over the rail while the sailors began to talk in subdued voices. Meg and John quietly joined their friend.

"What is it, Canso?" Meg could not help but ask.

For what seemed like a long time the big seaman did not reply. "It's difficult to explain," he said finally. "Since I met the two of you I have found myself thinking more and more about my home and the life I lead aboard ship. It is you who have made me see there is more to life than being a sailor. I left home so many years ago, and I was anxious to wander and discover the world, but now I find that I have nothing. I have worked aboard as many ships as there are countries that sail them. I have slaved for captains under good conditions and bad, but still I have nothing. Fifteen years before the mast and I have little more than the clothes on my back."

For a moment he was silent again.

"Fifteen years and then I get shanghaied aboard a ship that's so tender she should be recaulked and a cap'n that'll do nothing. The food is bad, they work us to the point of exhaustion and yet we can do nothing about it."

"Well, we must do something, Canso!" said Meg with sudden determination.

"But we can't, Meg," said John. "Be sensible."

"Don't talk to me like that, John Bains!" said Meg, very annoyed at her brother's superior attitude. "I found out that all you have to do is stand up to that captain and he'll give in. I told him how I was going to dress and he didn't do a thing about it."

"But Meg this is different. If we told him how to run his ship he'd just clap us in irons."

"You're afraid of him, John."

"We can't do anything. The cap'n would just say we're mutineers ...."

"Quiet now ... quiet before any of the officers hear us," ordered Canso, and he looked aft anxiously. "John's right, Meg. The cap'n won't listen to us. The man who complains will be held in irons for months."

"Then we're all just cowards. That's all!" And with that Meg stormed off the foredeck and went into her cabin in the aft of the ship.

The two sailors watched her go in silence. Finally Canso sighed and ran his fingers through his thick hair in frustration. "She just doesn't understand, John. We can't be telling the officers what to do or we'll find ourselves chained in the hold of this ship for the rest of the voyage." But the Nova Scotian sailor seemed upset by the argument, as if Meg had shown him how completely powerless he was.

As they sailed south it became hotter and hotter. For weeks the *Scotian* rolled lazily on long glassy swells, the sails hanging limp against the masts and the sun beating down with such intensity that the pitch bubbled out of the seams onto the deck. Everyone was relieved when they picked up the northeast trades somewhere south of Bermuda. The sails billowed and the ship began riding through the waves at nine or ten knots. The captain posted a constant watch on the foremast, and finally on a hot afternoon in late September the lookout shouted, "Land ho!"

They had sighted Hispaniola off the starboard bow. After navigating the Mona Passage, a course of due west was set and four days later the ship was under tow of a steam tug pulling them into the harbour of Kingston, Jamaica. Meg and John stood excitedly by the starboard foremast shrouds watching the dark green tropical island grow closer and closer to them. For the first time they were in a country that was totally foreign to their own Canadian homeland.

CHAPTER 7

"ANCHORS aweigh!" the captain shouted and the heavy iron anchors plopped into twenty-five feet of water. The ship glided forward with its own momentum until it got to the end of its chain and then slowly began swinging around.

John and Meg stood at the rail staring in fascination at the lush green tropical island that now surrounded them. They were morred in a huge harbour with blue water so clear that they could see fathoms down. The wharfs, stretching around for almost a mile, were ringed with a forest of sailing ships of every type and description, from heavy barques of over a thousand tons to small coastal schooners. The city of Kingston came right down to the water's edge and sprawled up the sides of the encircling mountains.

"All hands midships! All hands midships!" the captain called again.

The master stood with his back to the mainmast and the crew gathered around him. He was wearing his best dark blue jacket with polished brass buttons and a neat peaked cap, but his face was lined with strain and his eyes looked red and tired.

Before I go ashore I want you to know that we'll only be in port long enough to unload this cargo and take on another, if I can get one. I want every sailor among you to know that you're going to work for your money. Do you understand?"

Canso had been standing close to Meg and John. Now was his opportunity to say what had been bothering him. "Are we going to repair the hull, Cap'n?"

"What do you mean?"

"Now that we're in port, and we unload the cargo, we can roll her on her side and recaulk the hull."

"That's not a fit question for a sailor to ask, Canso, and you know it. I give the orders around here, and you'll obey. Do you understand?"

"You know this ship is tender, Cap'n," Canso said calmly. "You know better than any of us. If we go to sea in the shape she's in we'll be pumping all across the Atlantic."

"I'm the master of this ship and I decide how it's to be run!"

The captain looked from man to man, his fists doubled as if waiting for an attack. Then, finally, he looked back at the big Nova Scotian sailor.

"This argument is your fault, Canso. Because of it, I'm ordering that not a man aboard this ship will have liberty in this port."

"You can't do that," said Tommy, and many of the others were clearly upset. But the captain's anger was barely under control.

"I've heard enough from you men," he shouted. "You'll have no shore leave and that's the end of it. Now either get to work or you'll be flogged and clapped in irons!"

He paused for a moment. "I need two men to row me to the wharf. Since you've been doing all the talking Canso, you and your friend John Bains can just bend your backs by taking me ashore."

Within a few minutes the sailors had winched a lifeboat off the poop deck and into the sea. Canso, John and the captain climbed down the ladder and set out for shore. The two sailors sweltered in the tropical heat as they bent their backs to the oars. The captain sat in the stern, expressionless; occasionally his jaw worked to show he was still angry. As they neared shore the officer could contain himself no longer.

"I'm watching you closely, Canso, and don't forget it. If you should do anything ... anything at all that looks like insubordination, you'll get a taste of the type of discipline I can give out. Do you understand?"

The big sailor maintained the rhythm of the rowing without a pause and looked over the captain's head at the wispy white clouds without a hint of response in his face.

On the way back to the ship Canso expressed his bitter feelings to John. "I'll tell you boy, there'll be a day when the captain and I will settle our dispute."

In the late afternoon Captain Barnard was back on board ship. He gave the order to raise the anchor and before the men working the capstan had raised it above the surface of the water, a steam tug had arrived to tow the *Scotian* to a berth. By nightfall, just before the ebb of the tide, the ship was eased into a wharf and the lines were secured.

That evening Mr. Pepper made a big feast of the last of the salt pork and rice and for the first time in weeks the sailors were able to have tea made out of fresh water. After supper, Meg and John sat in the mess, and wrote a letter home to their mother, explaining everything that had happened to them. The next morning they would find a way to mail it to Canada. When they came out on deck the ship's company were lounging in the cool night air, smoking their pipes under the bright tropical stars and talking in groups.

Canso was usually the centre of attention but that evening he was very quiet. Finally Meg leaned over to him. "Are you still bothered by the argument, Canso?"

The big sailor stirred, glancing around to make sure the officers were out of earshot. "I tell you he can't hold us against our will. We've been on this hell ship for weeks eating rotten food. The cap'n's a slave driver."

"But there's nothing we can do," said John.

Canso suddenly stood up and addressed the crew. "We should skip ship. All of us at the same time. Let's see what he'd do then!" Lanterns on the ship and the wharf flickered dimly. It seemed deathly quiet. "Will anyone come with me? I'm sure there's a tavern close by. A drink would help us forget those weeks of eating duff and drinking rotten tea." But not a man moved. "Are none of you going to come? Are we not even going to stand up for ourselves?"

The sailors looked at their hands, or the decks. They looked everywhere except at Canso.

"I'll go," said Meg impulsively. "I don't care what the cap'n says."

John sat bolt upright. "Meg, you can't go to a tavern."

"Well I don't care. The cap'n can't tell us what to do all the time."

"Easy for you," said Joseph in his heavy Polish accent. "He's shown he'll never do anything to you, but the rest of us he'll clap in irons as soon as we get back aboard."

"Listen," said Canso. "Unless we do something we'll be sailing out of this harbour with the hull as tender as she is now and just the barest of provisions."

"Well, I'm not going to risk a flogging for a drink of rum," said Scobie.

"Me either," said another. All of the sailors seemed to agree.

Canso became silent. He could see that there was no way the crew were going to follow him.

The next day the hands were awakened early by the bosun. They finished breakfast well before dawn, then opened the hatches leading to the hold and the bow ports. Soon a crew of stevedores arrived and they set up a donkey on the wharf.

The donkey was a portable steam engine designed to winch heavy goods. It took an hour for the engineer to get the steam up on the machine. Meanwhile others set up a series of blocks on the forecastle head designed to lift the big timbers through the bow ports.

Finally they were ready to go. A cable was led from the winching drum of the donkey, through the series of blocks and into the hold via the bow ports. Inside the ship the sailors manhandled the heavy pieces of timber with peavey poles. Upon signal, the donkey started winding in the cable. Once it pulled on the piece of timber, the sailors had to guide it through the small opening of the bow ports.

It was dangerous work. The operator of the donkey could not see the men inside the ship. If the timber got stuck, the sailors would have to shout to someone outside who would signal the donkey driver to stop winching and give the cable some slack. The sailors would have to wrestle the log into position with their poles and then the winching could begin again. Once out of the ship, the timber would be swung up onto the wharf where wagons waited to haul them away to a nearby sawmill.

In spite of the hatches being removed, it was hot and uncomfortable for the sailors working in the hold of the ship. The stench of the bilge was nauseating and the rats scurried around for shelter. But the donkey was slow and awkward, giving the men long periods when they could loaf and chat.

John was posted as the signalman up on the jib boom, and from there he could watch the activities of the ships in the harbour, see the wagons coming back and forth to the wharf, and talk to the longshoremen. He developed an immediate liking for the black men, who spoke in soft voices.

Meg was one of the few people aboard ship who got ashore. Mr. Pepper was directed by the captain to buy provisions. He agreed to take Meg along, but only on the condition that she change into a dress. When she was ready, they set off with a hired wagon and driver.

The centre of Kingston was impressive, with broad avenues and big stone buildings. Palm trees lined the streets and there were flowers everywhere. It was exciting for Meg. Throngs of people of all races crowded the streets dressed in the most colourful clothes, but poverty seemed to be everywhere. The Chinese and East Indians were crammed into one poor section of the city and the black Africans occupied shanties in the rest of the city.

Everywhere they went, beggars ran after the wagon asking for a penny, and often they could see men engaged in heavy labour who were dressed in little more than rags. But the Europeans were obviously wealthy. More than once, as their wagon plodded through the streets, they passed magnificent carriages with matched pairs of horses and immaculately tailored servants. Inside, Meg could catch a glimpse of the white ladies and gentlemen going about their business or social affairs with an elegance that only the very rich could afford.

On the way into the store Mr. Pepper told Meg he intended to see to it that the crew would eat well on the outward bound voyage, and he stocked up with barrels of salt pork and cod, dried prunes, beans and bags of flour. With the help of the store employees they loaded their goods aboard the wagon and made their way back to the ship.

Captain Barnard saw them directing the stevedores where to store the provisions and he quickly called Mr. Pepper into his stateroom. Meg overheard some of the argument that broke out.

"Mr. Pepper," the captain was saying. "You must have spent a hundred dollars. I'm not a wealthy man."

Meg could see the cook through the doorway push his bowler hat back on his head and set his fists on his hips in a determined way. "If it's a voyage like the last one that ye'll be wantin' then you can find yerself another cook. Those sailors were hungry most of the time."

"I want to send most of that food back ...."

But Mr. Pepper must have won, for the next day, Meg saw that the provisions were stacked in the storage locker and that was the end of it. She was beginning to realize that the captain was sometimes willing to make concessions and that he was at times uncertain of himself.

It was Canso's concern about the condition of the ship that worried most of the seamen. The big Nova Scotian sailor talked about it incessantly as if he could think of nothing else. As the timber was unloaded out of the hold, the men would examine the wooden hull. Almost everywhere they looked below the waterline, traces could be seen where the water had seeped through the seams. The bosun had them slather tar on the boards inside the hull but everyone knew that the only real answer was to pull the *Scotian* out of the water and recaulk the hull with pitch and oakum.

Not long after they had docked, the Captain disappeared on shore. When he returned two days later, the rumour quickly spread that they would be taking on a load of sugar cane destined for Liverpool, England.

There was no mention of the repairs that needed to be done on the hull.

Canso urged the other sailors to try to do something about the condition of the ship, but they ignored him and even felt uneasy talking about it.

Only Meg and John listened to the complaints of the big sailor and this seemed to draw the three of them closer together.

Within a few days they finished unloading the rest of the timbers. Then, at high tide, a small steam tug came alongside and when a rope was secured, the moorings were loosened and the ship was pulled across the bay to the ballast pile.

When windjammers were empty or carrying a light cargo, they had to fill their holds with a ballast of rocks for stability. Otherwise they ran the risk of capsizing in the first strong wind. In every port there would be piles of ballast rock where ships would dump or take on ballast depending on whether they were to carry a heavy or light cargo. The *Scotian* was to carry sugar cane to Liverpool, and because it was light, the ship would need extra weight in her hold.

Loading ballast was terrible work for the sailors. A gang was put ashore and they started loading canvas slings full of rock. A boom was rigged up on the mainmast and when the sling was filled, it would be winched up by hand, swung over the side of the ship and lowered into the hold through the main hatch. The rocks were jagged and heavy and tore at their clothing. It was even worse for the sailors down in the hold. They had to shift the rocks by hand to keep them evenly distributed. It took five days of back-breaking work before the captain decided there was enough weight in the ship.

Again they had to lift the anchor with the capstan, and a tug towed them across to a wharf where sugar cane was waiting to be loaded. The stevedores that were hired walked up a narrow gangway aboard ship with a huge pile of cane weighing anywhere up to one hundred pounds. When they got to the open hatchway, they dropped it down into the hold. For the sailors down below it was miserable work. They had to wrestle with the bulky sugar cane and store it compactly in the hold. All day they had to scramble over the jagged pieces of rock ballast, often skinning their hands and knees. The sticky sweet syrup oozed out of the cane and got in their hair and all over their clothes.

The night they finished loading the square-rigger the seamen were gathered out on the main deck relaxing before they turned in to sleep. The captain had already announced that they would be sailing with the morning's tide.

Canso stood by himself, leaning against the rail which overlooked the wharf. He caught John's eye and motioned for him and Meg to come over to talk. He seemed pale and nervous in the flickering lantern light, as if he were anxious about something.

"I want the two of you to help me," he whispered. "You're the only ones I can really trust. I've decided to desert ship."

"You mean you're going to leave?" Meg asked in disbelief.

"I can't stand it anymore, Meg. The cap'n won't listen to reason. He's going to take this ship down and everyone with it. But he's not going to get me. If I can get off tonight he won't have time to find me before the ship sails tomorrow."

"But you can't just leave us here, Canso."

"I've got to."

Meg pulled at the sailor's sleeve. "Take us with you."

"How can I do that?"

"We can all get a passage aboard a ship to Canada. Then John and I can make our way back to Ottawa."

"I can't, Meg. Don't you understand? It'll be hard enough for me to get a ship out of this port. If I was to take the two of you we may never get off the beach."

"But you can't just leave us here, Canso," she pleaded.

"No! I can't stay. Try to understand." Canso knit his brow in an effort to explain. "A sailor lives his life alone. He's got to look after himself. Someday, maybe you'll understand."

The three stood in the darkness for what seemed to be a long time without saying a word. John studied the Nova Scotian seaman who had become such a close friend in those few weeks. The boy so desperately wanted to desert the ship and be with Canso, but he knew that the sailor was right. There would be the chance for only one of them to desert. "We understand Canso," he said, but the disappointment sounded in his voice. "If you want to get off the ship, we'll help you."

Canso nodded and got down to business. "Now, I've got to put a rope over the side of the ship so I can get away. What I need is someone to pull it back up once I'm gone. And I need another person to talk to the officers so they are distracted."

The three talked in low voices until the plans were finally settled. Then John went to the poop deck. The others waited until he was talking to the officers. Canso got the rope that he had stashed, tied it to the rail, and softly let it over the side. He glanced toward the officers and in a moment was up and over the rail.

"Goodbye Meg," he whispered. "I hope you don't feel bad about me."

Then he was gone.

Meg leaned up against the rope to conceal it and watched the poop deck. She could hear Canso lower himself, then swing out until he caught the edge of the wharf. The rope thumped back against the hull of the ship as he let it fall, and there was the sound of feet running on the gravel-surfaced wharf.

Suddenly he was discovered. "A deserter! A deserter! Cap'n, a deserter!" It was the mate shouting at the top of his voice. The captain was on deck in an instant. The bosun and the mate were running down the rail.

"Look, a rope!" shouted the mate. "And you, Meg. You were trying to cover it up. And your brother was in on it too!"

The captain was pulling on his blue coat. "Who's missing?"

"I don't know sir, but I'll lay odds it's Canso."

A moment later the mate had searched the crew and confirmed his suspicions.

"I'll go after him," said the captain. "And keep an eye on those two Bains kids. I'll want to talk to them when I get back." In a moment the captain was over the side and gone.

CHAPTER 8

TWO hours later the captain returned. He seemed exhausted. His coat was unbuttoned, and sweat darkened his hair, trickling down his face and into his beard. The mate quickly went down the gangway and helped him aboard.

"I chased him down streets and alleys, but he was too fast for me," said the captain, pausing to rest. He seemed old and tired. "I even called out for him to stop, but he just ran like the wind."

All of the sailors had stayed on deck tensely waiting to hear the outcome of the chase. The master stiffened when he saw them watching and listening to him. He gathered himself together and his hand came up and pointed at them in an accusing way. "Let me tell every man here that I'm not finished with Mr. Canso. No Bluenose skipper like me was ever beaten by a man living in the fo'c's'le head. Someday I'll find him and he'll pay his dues. You mark my word!"

The lantern hanging on the mainmast flickered dimly in the master's face making him appear pale and ghostlike. Suddenly he was tired; his head sagged and he walked slowly to his cabin at the after section of the ship. The young mate put out his hand to help him but he instinctively shook it off. "Leave me alone!" he said crossly.

When he got near the entrance to the cabins, the captain stopped. "Mr. McKenzie."

"Aye, sir."

"Bring the brother and sister to see me in fifteen minutes."

"Aye, sir."

Both Meg and John stiffened. They were terrified. Never before had they seen the captain so upset. What would he do to them? The fifteen minutes seemed to pass like hours. They stood, looking out across the bay. The crew wanted to give them encouragement but not one could find a thing to say. The longer they waited, the more tense they became, so that in the end it was all they could do to control themselves.

Finally the mate called from the darkened poop deck. "John, Meg, the captain will see you now."

They stumbled through the dark until they found the mate waiting by the captain's door. He pushed it open. Meg and John stepped inside and the mate came in behind.

The captain sat at his mahogany desk. A candle flickered at his left hand, showing his pale face and moist brow. His jacket hung open and his white, starched shirt was stained with sweat. In front of him stood a bottle of rum and a half-filled tumbler.

As he looked up at them, he brushed his hand nervously through his beard. "So you helped Canso desert, did you? I suppose you're proud of your work."

The captain paused, waiting for a response. "Are you?" he demanded sharply.

"No … no sir," John managed to get out. The boy was prepared for the worst. They had broken the law of the sea and he knew they would be punished.

The captain took a drink. His eyes were a little glazed. "How long have you been planning this?"

"Just tonight, sir."

The master leaned toward them. "Were the two of you going to go with him?"

"No sir, we weren't, really," Meg said quickly.

"It looks like it to me. You were down by the rail with him, weren't you Meg? You were going to slip over the side after Canso got away and then John would go next. Isn't that right?"

"No sir," John said firmly. "We helped Canso but we weren't going to go ourselves."

"That's what you say now, after you got caught, but I know how you think. I know what goes on in a fo'c's'le. You all want to desert. Isn't that true? Well, I can tell you that you've signed on for the full trip back to a Canadian port and I'll keep you to your word."

The captain's intensity made him breathless. The lantern was flickering in his pale face and beads of sweat stood out on his brow. He took a swig of rum, almost gagging on its sharp taste, and then he continued.

"I don't care if you do hate me. What Canso did was wrong! Wrong, do you hear me? What's worse is that I need a man like him. He has the strength and skill of five sailors. Damn you, Canso!" And the captain pounded the desk with his fist, making the bottle and glass jump.

A moment later he had buried his head in his hands and was muttering to himself in a low, desperate voice, as if in a drunken stupor. "Things are within my grasp now. I've worked all my life to be a master and to own my own ship, but now that I have it everything seems to go wrong. The banks tell me they want their money back. Then I have to scramble to get a cargo … they pay me so little I can barely make a profit … the ship's tender … she's taking on water almost as fast as we can pump it out of her. What can I do? I'm a ruined man."

John and Meg had not moved from their positions. They stared at the captain, shocked to find him telling them this. The master finished what was in his glass and then refilled it, almost ignoring their presence.

"I'm tired of all of this," he continued. "I've worked and struggled all of my life. I went to sea as a boy of twelve, learning in the fo'c's'le with all the other hands. Since then I've survived many a hardship. I became a third mate, then second and first until I had my own command. Now I even have my own ship."

The captain was suddenly aware that he was not alone.

"I'll not lose my ship because a man like Canso deserts. You'll pay for your crimes, every one of you," he said angrily. He drank again and then looked at them out of bloodshot, bleary eyes. "I have to think of a punishment fit for the two of you. If I was to give you the rope's end I'd have every sailor aboard ship angry with me, but they must know that Cap'n Barnard is not to be defied."

Meg and John glanced uneasily at each other.

"I have only one alternative then," he continued, slurring his words. "I'll put you in irons for the rest of the night. That way we can be sure that you won't desert and it'll be a fitting punishment. What do you think, eh?"

A nod was as much as either John or Meg could muster.

"You should thank me that it's not worse. Take them to the hold, Mr. McKenzie, and shackle them there until dawn."

"Aye, sir."

As John and Meg walked slowly across the main deck, the mate tried to give them an explanation. "You've got to understand the cap'n. He's not a bad man. He has to deliver his cargo or go bankrupt, and he needs the entire crew to do it. He's worried about what will happen now that Canso's gone. We all depended on him."

John stopped. "Do we really have to go down into the hold, Mr. McKenzie?"

"Those were the cap'n's orders."

"But it's dirty," Meg added. "And there's rats and spiders and everything among the sugar cane."

"Count yourself lucky, girl. I've seen masters hand out discipline worse than that by far."

The whole ship's company were waiting to learn what had happened. A pale lantern light showed the concern on their faces. José came forward as they approached. "What sentence did he give?"

"He ordered them into irons until dawn."

"He can't do that. They're too young."

"He can't blame them for what Canso did," said Hans. "It's not fair."

"You're not going to carry it out are you, Mr. McKenzie?"

Eight angry sailors faced the young mate, who was flanked by Meg and John. There was sharp hostility in the air.

"I have to carry out the punishment. It was laid down by the captain."

"But …."

"That'll be all," said the mate firmly. "You men get back to the fo'c's'le and leave this business to me."

The sailors were uncertain what to do. They glanced uneasily at each other as if looking for someone to give leadership but no one came forward. The mate pushed his way through the group until he came to the hatch leading to the hold. He threw it open, and then, taking the lantern from the mainmast, he began his descent into the blackness.

"John, Meg, you follow me," he ordered.

The two of them stood at the edge of the hatch watching him disappear. John grasped his sister's hand for reassurance, then put his foot on the top rung of the ladder and slowly followed the mate. The mate stood at the bottom of the ladder on top of the sharp sticks of sugar cane, holding the lantern up so the others could see. The light flickered into the dark corners of the hold, showing uneven mounds of cane and ribs and beams of the ship.

A couple of minutes later both John and Meg were shackled around the ankles and wrists with heavy chains winding around the beams so they could not stand up. When he had finished, the mate took the lantern. "I'll be down to free you at first light," he said, and then carefully he made his way over to the ladder.

Meg and John watched the dim lantern light slowly disappear up the ladder to the deck. With a loud bang the hatch slammed shut and they were in complete and total darkness. For a moment they heard footsteps above their heads, then silence.

All of their senses became sharply acute. They could feel the slight bobbing of the ship as it gently rode at its moorings. The vile smell of the bilge was mixed with the sweet odour of the sugar cane. They could see absolutely nothing. It was as if they had been struck blind and were lost in a strange place without any bearings. It was suffocating.

"I'm scared," Meg said.

"We've got to try and be calm." But the boy was far from controlling himself. "At least we've got each other." As they talked, their chains rattled with each movement, and the noise seemed to give some reassurance.

They were quiet for a few moments, trying to adjust to their new surroundings. Suddenly there was a rustling close by.

"Was that you?" Meg asked anxiously.

"No."

They strained to hear. The rustling was clearer now. They heard movements over to their left and then there was a noise at the other side of the ship. The rustling was all about them.

"Rats!" whispered John and panic rose in his voice. "The rats are everywhere. They're all around us!"

"Go away!" Meg shouted suddenly. "Get away from here!" Her movements rattled the chain noisily, and then John joined her by clanking his chains as loudly as possible.

For two or three minutes they kept up the noise, but slowly they grew tired and stopped. Their ears strained. There was not a sound. Then there was a rustling. There was a scurrying of little feet close by. Farther off there was more noise. It was all around them again.

"Kick at them! Hit them! Do anything!"

The dark gave them a sense of helplessness which drove them close to terror. John pulled at a piece of sugar cane to use as a weapon but he could not get it free. Meg crouched on her haunches, her fists clenched, waiting for something to attack her.

"Can you hold onto my hand?" John said reaching out to his sister. The two of them groped in the darkness until they found each other. Now at least they had evidence that the other existed.

"This is terrible," said John bitterly. "The cap'n should know better than to send people down here."

"He's gone mad, John. That's what it is."

"I don't think so, Meg. It's the law of the sea. He has the right to discipline us any way he sees fit, but he shouldn't go this far." There was a long pause as the boy considered their situation. "We've got to oppose him, Meg. Anyone who would run a ship the way he's done is not fit for a command."

Meg could tell from the determined quality in her brother's voice that his mind was made up and that something was bound to result. But now the two of them were very tired. In the last few days they had worked very strenuously, and it had been hours since they had had any sleep. Every time they began to relax, the rats resumed their restless activity. Once John leaned back against the ship's hull and tried to tell stories as a way of passing time, but then he heard something a few inches from his head. He gave a frightened sharp scream, kicking out in the direction of the noise, but it was gone. Gradually they settled back again, and exhaustion slowly got the better of them. Somehow, they dozed off.

They were both asleep when the hatch was suddenly ripped open and the light of the early morning dawn came flooding into the hold. A moment later the mate was beside them opening the shackles that held their wrists and ankles.

"Were you all right?" the mate asked anxiously.

Meg was rubbing her wrists. "This is hardly the most comfortable berth aboard ship."

When they were above deck, the sailors crowded around asking about their ordeal, but the mate moved them on. "Breakfast now. Let's get going. The tug will be here within the hour."

John and Meg were still half asleep, but they forced themselves to eat. Afterwards they went back on deck.

The mate and bosun were shouting orders to crew members in preparation for departure. The captain appeared and began to pace the poop deck restlessly. His face, and particularly the look about his eyes, had a brooding quality as if the alcohol and the events of the last day made him unsteady and uncertain about his command. The sun was over the horizon bringing warmth and new life. It slanted through the forest of masts and spars of ships cramming the wharfs and brought a deep blue colour to the water of the harbour and a dark green to the hillsides. Things seemed alive and active again.

Suddenly there was a man on the wharf. "Cap'n! Cap'n!" the mate was shouting. "Look, it's Canso!"

The captain ran to midships. "Get him! Don't let him get away! Put out the gangplank! You men get down onto the wharf!"

But Canso did not stir. He stood with his hands on his hips. His dark seaman's clothing hung loosely on his huge frame, and his peaked sailor's cap was pulled over his forehead. He stared defiantly at the captain without a movement.

"Get the gangway out!" the master shouted excitedly and when it was finally out, he scrambled down it as fast as he could go, with the mate and bosun behind. "We've got you!" he shouted in triumph.

Canso made no effort to move until the captain tried to grab his arm. The big seaman shook it off. "Leave me! I have returned on my own. I'll go aboard ship by myself."

"Get him before he gets away," shouted the captain.

"I will go myself. Keep your hands to yourself." Canso said it in such a threatening way that the others dared not touch him. The big man walked up the gangway of the ship, pausing long enough to smile shyly at his crew mates, and particularly at John and Meg.

"Take him below, Mr. McKenzie," ordered the captain. "Put him in irons and I'll deal with him when we're at sea."

1. Shipping and shipbuilding was one of the most important industries in Maritime Canada throughout the nineteenth century. The average ship, like the one in this photo, was a three-masted vessel with square-rigged sails on all three masts.

2. There were hundreds of small ports in the three Maritime provinces and those parts of Québec where ships were built. This photo shows planking on the hull of a half-finished ship. The steam is escaping from the small hut in the background where the timbers were heated and bent into shape. The peak year for the Canadian shipping industry was 1878 when the country stood fifth on the list of ship-owning nations of the world. After 1880, the shipping industry went into rapid decline as the wooden-hulled ships became obsolete and steel hulls became the rule.

3. Repairs to wooden-hulled ships were constantly needed or they would begin to leak. This ship has been rolled on its side so that the hull can be made watertight by recaulking the seams.

4. The design of ships has always been changing and adapting to meet new needs. In the 1850's, clipper ships that were sharp in the bow and narrow in the beam became the rule, but in the latter part of the century, as steamers took over the fast passages, the square-rigged sailing ship was designed to carry heavy bulk cargos. This ship is called a barque. Characteristic of this design are the square-rigged sails on the fore and main masts and what were called fore-and-aft rigged sails on its mizzen mast.

5. This is a four-masted barque under full sail. The sharp bow is a characteristic of the clipper ships.

6. As the sailing ships declined in importance towards the latter part of the nineteenth century, some shipbuilders innovated with new ship designs. This steel-hulled four-masted schooner was probably owned by an American company, but the photo was taken in the Strait of Canso, Nova Scotia.

7. This picture of St. John, New Brunswick shows the forest of masts characteristic of any busy harbour during this period. The tugs in the foreground were used to tow the wind-driven ships in and out of the harbour.

8. The crew aboard a Nova Scotian square-rigged ship faced a life of constant hardship and danger. In this picture, the captain, his wife, and officers are in the back row and the crew of eight are in the foreground. The common practice in this era was that the officers were drawn from the ship's home country but the crew were hired in any port where they could be found. In spite of low pay, poor food, hard work, and often brutal discipline, many men seemed content to spend a lifetime at sea.

9. This picture of a captain on the poop deck of his ship shows some of the fine details that were built into these wooden vessels. The sky-light gives ventilation and light to the cabins, which were immediately below deck. The upright stand with the glass window on it is the binnacle which holds the compass.

10. Although the crew of ships lived in primitive conditions in the forecastle, this picture of a captain's cabin shows that the master enjoyed comfortable and even luxurious surroundings.

11. The Canadian shipping industry was greatly stimulated in the last century by the timber trade. This picture shows ships being loaded with squared logs, which were most likely cut in the Upper Ottawa River Valley and floated downriver in enormous log rafts to Québec City. Every year, from July through the freeze-up in late fall, ships would gather in Québec to take on timber for the British and West Indian markets.

12. Timber was by no means the only cargo of Canadian ships. Here an old wooden sailing ship is unloading coal into box cars.

13. Once inside the ship, the timber would be stored bottom of the hold. This unusual picture, taken inside a wooden ship in 1872, not only shows the cargo but also clearly illustrates the curve of the hull and the ribs and beams supporting the vessel.

14. One of the most frequently travelled routes of Canadian cargo ships in the last century involved taking timber to Britain and returning back to Canada filled with emigrants. The vast majority of the people coming to this continent at this time travelled steerage class under terrible conditions. The voyage normally lasted from eight to ten weeks. During storms the emigrants were forced to stay below where there was virtually no ventilation. Drinking water often became bad, and epidemics of cholera, dysentery and smallpox frequently were rampant. This woodcut, published in the *Illustrated London News* in 1850, shows the emigrants in happier times dancing in their quarters.

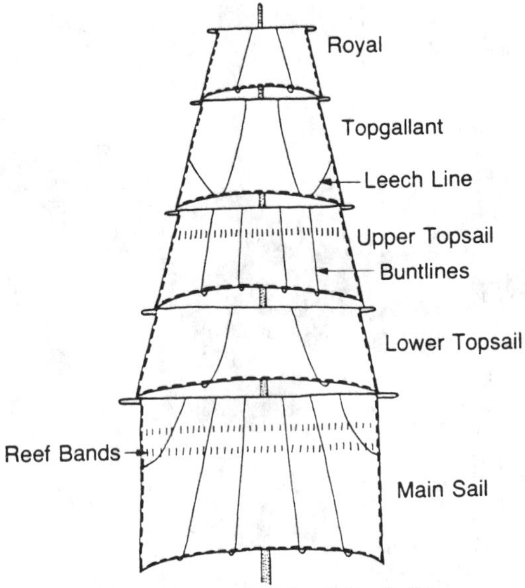

The Forward Side of the Sails

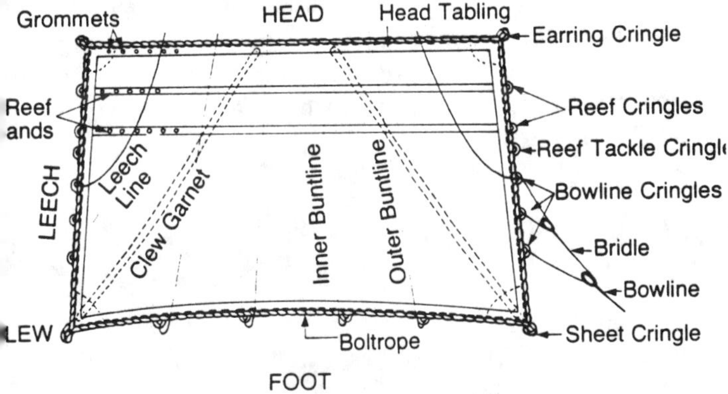

Detail of a Course on a Ship of 1800

15. A square-rigged sailing ship took a tremendous amount of physical work to keep in good running order. Part of the watch, in this picture, are pulling on the lee fore brace to trim the sails.

16. When the weather was settled the sailors were often put to work cutting and sewing sails.

17 and 18. Work aloft was the most dangerous chore aboard ship. As the sailors stretched themselves out along the yard arm to stow or set a sail they would spread their feet along the stirrups and clutch onto the yard arm for support.

19. Once the weather turned bad, to be aloft meant a sailor took his life in his hands.

20. During a storm, if a sailor was to misplace his foot or lose his grip on the yard, he could be tossed out into space and lost at sea.

21. Under normal conditions, to handle the ship's wheel was one of the most pleasant chores but in heavy seas it could take all the strength of two sailors to manage.

22. During a storm the ship would plunge back and forth with such violence that the sea would wash on deck. Lifelines had to be strung along the rail for the sailors to hold, or they could be swept overboard.

23. Shipwrecks were common in the last century. In August, 1873, over a thousand Canadian sailors were lost in one storm alone. Once a ship began to go down or was crushed on rocks, the chances of survival were slim. This ship in the picture seems to be more fortunate than most. It has washed up on a sandy shore and the crew are struggling to get her secure.

CHAPTER 9

THE steam tug had the *Scotian* under tow, slowly pulling her out of Kingston harbour toward the open sea. The sailors were relaxing on the main deck in the hot tropical sun watching the city recede and waiting for the order to set sail.

It took only a few moments for Meg and John to realize that the way was clear for them to slip down into the hold to see Canso, unnoticed by any of the officers. The big sailor had been sitting in the pool of sunlight that came through the hatchway. As they came down the ladder he gave them both a warm embrace.

The rough seaman seemed deeply moved by the reunion. "It's good to be back aboard," he said happily.

"It's good to have you back," said Meg. "We thought you were gone forever," added John. "I almost was," said Canso.

The three relaxed comfortably on the sugar cane. All of the terror that Meg and John associated with the place was gone now that Canso was there and the sunlight was coming through the hatchway.

"How come you're not in irons?" the boy asked suddenly.

Canso smiled. "I think the mate couldn't bring himself to do it," he said.

"Well he shouldn't," said Meg. "After all, you came back yourself."

Canso nodded.

"Why did you come back, Canso?" asked John.

The big seaman was quiet for a few moments as he considered what to say. "It's difficult to explain. I never would have been caught. When the captain spotted me, I ran and ran. He couldn't have caught me in three nights. But as soon as I was free, I began to feel guilty. I came to see what I had done was abandon you."

Canso's voice was hushed and his words carefully chosen. "You see, last night when I jumped ship I asked you both to help me — to sacrifice yourselves for me — but I wasn't willing to do anything in return. Do you understand what that means? I was deserting you. I was leaving you aboard ship to face the hardships alone while I went off to save myself."

The sun slanted down through the open hatchway, shining directly on the features of Canso's face. "I had to return to the ship. It was the only way that I could show that I was worthwhile."

Meg nodded solemnly and John answered, "Whatever the reasons, Canso, we're glad to have you back. It makes us feel so much better."

As they chatted they could feel the *Scotian* begin to pitch into the waves and they knew that they were in the open sea. Soon the mate was shouting, "Stand by to cast off the towrope!" Then a moment later they heard: "Cast off." The ship was drifting free on a calm, glassy sea.

Again the mate was shouting. "All hands set sail! All hands set sail!"

"I've got to go," John said as he made for the ladder. "Are you coming, Canso?"

"I'm to wait here for the cap'n's orders."

It did not take long for the seamen to unfurl the sails. A course of due east was set. As the big ship's canvas filled with the northwest wind, the *Scotian* leaned slightly over on her starboard beam and began slicing through the waves at a speed of five or six knots. By the time the crew had finished, the island of Jamaica was slowly receding behind them. It was approaching mid-day and the hot tropical sun streamed steadily out of a clear blue sky, making the deck hot to touch. Already the sailors were sweltering and they stripped their shirts.

The captain was still in his quarters. The mate stood near the helmsman, spending a long time consulting the charts and checking their course. The bosun was forward, coiling ropes as if trying to find something to do. The crew were left on their own, waiting in the hot sun for the discipline to begin.

Finally the captain emerged from his quarters and climbed up the ladder to the poop deck. In spite of the heat he was wearing his dark blue jacket with the brass buttons done up to his neck. His face was flushed and his eyes red. He stood stiffly, with one hand on the rail, as if he needed support to steady himself. The crew stopped talking the moment the master appeared and they watched his every move. He waited for a long time, staring at the crew gathered on the main deck, touching the poop rail lightly with his hand.

"Bring up Canso, Mr. Mckenzie," he said suddenly, but his voice was weak and irresolute.

"Aye, sir." Swiftly the mate went down the ladder into the hold; a moment later he reappeared, followed by the big Nova Scotian sailor.

The captain came down to midships and met them on the burning hot deck. Canso appeared amazingly calm for someone about to receive harsh punishment. The captain was nervous, looking anxiously from sailor to sailor as if trying to gauge what they were thinking.

As he spoke, the captain's voice faltered, but then became stronger. "You … you're a deserter, Canso. A deserter. You know what that means."

The big man nodded.

"I have given this much thought, and I have decided that I must discipline you. Make an example of you, so that any others who might think of doing the same will know the punishment they will receive. Do you understand?"

"I understand, Captain." Canso did not move.

"You're to be hung from the mizzen yard by your wrists and given twenty lashes of a greased rope."

The sailors stiffened. José and Tommy stepped forward as if they were about to intervene. Others murmured under their breath.

"You can't do that, Cap'n!" John said suddenly. "Canso came back by himself. He could have stayed away, and you'd never have caught him."

"He's a deserter," said the captain, astounded at a young boy daring to speak that way to him. "He deserves punishment."

"No," John insisted. "You're not being fair."

"Who's to say whether I'm fair or not? I am the captain of this ship. My word is law for all who sail on her."

"It's not fair! Canso came back by himself." Both the mate and the bosun tried to shush John but he was so upset he would not be quiet. "If you discipline Canso it will be an injustice!" shouted the boy.

The captain turned on John, a menacing expression on his face. "I tell you, boy, that I am the master of this ship. Only I will decide how she will be run and what discipline is to be meted out. I'll not have you or any other member of this crew interfering. The sentence is hanging from the mizzen yard and twenty lashes of the rope. If there's any more talk from the likes of you, you'll be joining him. Is that clear?"

The crew stood stony-faced and sullen. John looked from face to face, hoping to find someone who might support him, but Meg seemed the only one who was not afraid to show the same anger as himself. Meanwhile, the captain continued with the job at hand.

"Mr. Mckenzie, Mr. Ryerson, bring the prisoner aft with you." Nervously, the captain wiped perspiration from his face and began to unbutton the heavy wool jacket he was wearing. "Well, can't you hear? I said, bring the prisoner aft!"

The officers went to grasp Canso's arms, but he pulled away. "I'll go myself," he said proudly.

The crew gathered on the poop deck as the captain tied Canso's wrists together with a strong rope. The sailor had taken off his shirt to keep cool in the searing heat, and already the sweat had gathered on his heavily muscled chest, running in rivulets down his back. He was calm, as if storing up his strength to withstand the impending ordeal.

After tying Canso's wrists the captain led the rope through a block on the mizzen yard, eight or nine feet above the deck, and then through another on the mast. He held onto the coiled end of the rope and motioned to Tommy and José who were standing by the larboard rail. "You!" he ordered. "Come and pull Canso up." Neither of them moved. "I said come and pull him up. That's an order!" But both sailors stared back at their captain without a hint of emotion on their faces.

The captain turned to the others who were encircling him. Georges stood near the mast. "Pull him up!" the captain shouted, motioning to the coiled rope. Georges did not move.

"You, Hans! Pull Canso up. I order you." But the Dutch sailor's only reaction was a scowl.

The captain was in a frenzy. The sweat ran off him in torrents and he tore off his heavy jacket. The white starched shirt that he wore underneath was soaked. "This is mutiny! You know that!" the captain shouted hoarsely. "When you're given an order by your master, you must carry it out. Those are the rules of the sea!"

He looked urgently from man to man but no one stirred. Suddenly Mr. Mckenzie stepped forward and took the coiled rope from the captain's hand. His face was pale and grim as if he loathed the job and was doing it only out of a sense of duty. Without looking at Canso, he steadied himself near the mast and pulled on the rope. But the sailor was too heavy for the mate. The bosun joined in to help and even the captain pulled on the end of the rope. Finally Canso was pulled off the deck and hung suspended in the air. With a quick motion the mate tied the rope off.

The sailor was now suspended by his wrists four inches above the deck. Each time the *Scotian* pitched into a wave, his body swung backwards; it came forward as the ship slipped into the trough. The crew and the officers waited tensely for something to happen. Minutes passed without a word being spoken; everyone was transfixed by the swaying motion of the body and the tension in the air.

The sun beat down unmercifully. There was not a breath of cooling air. At first Canso withstood the punishment easily, but after five minutes his body was a deep red colour and dripped with sweat. Within ten minutes the pain was making his eyes close tight. A few minutes later, his breath wheezed out in gasps and his head hung.

John was beside himself. The captain had to take Canso down, he thought, before there was permanent damage. It was not fair. Canso had returned to the ship by himself. The captain was disciplining him only because he had been made to look foolish. He must stop.

The captain positioned himself a pace away from the sailor's swaying body, clutching a six-foot length of rope which was heavily greased at one end. All the colour had drained from his face and his hair was matted with sweat. He seemed determined to carry out the sentence.

Canso seemed close to losing consciousness now; his eyes were glazed and his head lolled onto his chest. The captain steadied himself, his arm raised, ready to strike at the naked back.

"No!" shouted John. "You can't do it, Captain!" He could not stand it any longer. "You're not going to carry out the sentence!"

John took a step toward his master. He was threatening now in a way that was a real challenge to the captain's authority. John realized it was mutiny, but he did not care any more.

"Put that rope down now!" John yelled.

Captain Barnard seemed confused. "Keep away! Keep back. It is a crime to oppose the captain's command!"

"It's not fair to flog Canso. He did nothing wrong, Captain." John was decisive. His eyes and the set of his jaw showed he would not back down. The other sailors had moved forward, willing to follow the boy's leadership.

"Keep back! All of you. Keep back! This is mutiny. I have the right to carry out my sentence. It is the law of the sea!" But the desperation marking his voice showed that the captain was quickly losing control.

"Drop the rope, Captain." John ordered again. "Canso has been disciplined enough."

"He must be flogged!"

"No!" John shouted with a cold firmness that indicated he meant what he said. "A captain's job is to control his ship, not drive his sailors to desert. Flogging is not the way to run a ship. Our welfare is your responsibility. You are not doing your job."

The captain took a step toward John as if to whip the boy with his greased rope, but his knees were trembling and he stumbled. With wide eyes, he looked from sailor to sailor, but they only stared back at him, grim and determined. The rope slid out of his hand as he wiped sweat from the corners of his eyes, which were bloodshot from too much drinking.

"If you want this ship to reach port," John said quietly, "you'll have to treat us like human beings."

"Don't you dare ..." the captain began, but then, defeated, he turned away from the accusing eyes of the crew. When he spoke again, his voice was barely audible. "Cut him down."

The sailors were silent, astonished at their victory. "Damn you, cut him down," ordered the captain sharply. "And have done with it." Then he scooped up the rope and hurried away with long strides toward his cabin.

"Cut him down!" John repeated excitedly. "Cut him down!" A moment later the rope went slack and Canso's heavy body was eased onto the deck by the seamen. Mr. Pepper was running for water, and others were mopping the sweat from Canso's exhausted body.

"We did it!" Tommy exclaimed. "The captain had to give in to us!"

Meg was excited. “You were the one that did it, John,” and she hugged her older brother out of sheer joy.

Canso was conscious now. He looked up at his shipmates and then with an effort reached his hand up to John’s shoulder and smiled.

“Thank you, boy. It’s a true sailor that stands up for his mates and puts his own life on the line. I’ll not forget it.”

CHAPTER 10

THE voyage of the *Scotian* from Jamaica to Liverpool was a bitter affair. Captain Barnard seemed to cut off all communication with everyone on the ship. For hours he paced the poop deck near the helmsman, avoiding the looks of his crew, and talking only to bark out commands in an angry manner. In time his face developed a haggard, exhausted look as if he had pushed himself beyond his limit.

The crew reacted with a sullen resentfulness which they did not try to hide. There was constant grumbling about their treatment, the food, and the continual work. Meg noticed that rarely did the men sing their work shanties anymore or gather on the foredeck in the evening to dance a version of the hornpipe. It was as if the disciplining of Canso and John's rebellion against the captain had drawn the lines between the officers and crew so sharply that there was no more room for understanding or good times aboard the ship.

Strangely it was Canso who was now more sympathetic to the captain than any of the others. Often when the complaints of the seamen reached their bitterest, he would say that the master was under a lot of pressure to get paid for his cargo or that he was doing the best he could under the circumstances. When John or Meg tried to talk to the big seaman about it, he would only shrug and make some meaningless comment. They felt that he had drifted away from them to take the captain's side completely, but they could not understand why.

The condition of the ship seemed to deteriorate with every day of the passage. More than once a canvas sail, worn thin from years of use, would split into ribbons as it backed out against a mast, and on one occasion, when a strong westerly wind was blowing, a sudden strong gust snapped the maintop mast stay. In rapid succession the main and mizzen stays gave away. It was only through good seamanship on the part of the captain and daring work in the rigging by the entire crew that they were able to avoid a complete demasting. It was the constant pumping, however, that the sailors resented most of all. At least ten hours out of every day the crew had to man the pump to keep the ship dry. The heavy physical work took its toll on the men, leaving their muscles aching.

But in spite of the rough crossing, the *Scotian* rode the heavy seas like a true clipper. They were seven weeks out of Kingston, driving before a wet southwest wind, when the captain posted a lookout at the ship's prow. It was getting toward dusk when there was a shout of "Land ho!" They had sighted the southern coast of Ireland. Three days later they were under tow into Liverpool harbour.

As they came into the harbour, all the crew crowded on the foredeck. Meg and John were beside Canso, and the Nova Scotian sailor pointed out an incredible variety of ships and read out the company flags flying from their mainmasts. Liverpool, situated at the mouth of the Mersey River, was Britain's largest and busiest port, and that day her harbour was filled with every imaginable type of ship.

There were iron-plated steamers, still carrying square-rigged sails, that made regular runs to Québec, New York, Boston, the West Indies and South America. There were hundreds of square-rigged ships that sailed to Africa, India, Australia, and the Far East. Some of the ships were sleek three- and four-masted clippers with huge masts and yards which could spread acres of canvas to the winds, while others were broad-beamed ships and barques designed to carry heavy loads across long distances. There were wool ships from Australia and timber droghers from Québec, tea clippers that ran to China and white-stained guano ships that regularly traded with South America. There were small schooners engaged in coastal trade, tugs for working around the harbour and ferries to take passengers from one side of the harbour to the other.

Into Merseyside came imports from around the world. Raw cotton from the southern United States and India; wool from Australia; tea from India, Ceylon and China; sugar and spices from both the East and West Indies; and timber and cod from Canada. Outbound from the harbour went millions of yards of cotton cloth manufactured in the the Lancashire mills, rock salt, coal, iron bars, machinery and every imaginable type of manufactured good.

When they were going past the ships of the Black Ball Line, Canso suddenly shouted. "Look, look everybody! It's the *Marco Polo*." All the crew strained to get a good view of one of the most famous of all the clippers. She was old now, built in New Brunswick in 1851, and her wooden hull was getting tender, but for some time her record voyages to Australia had made news with every trip. On one occasion, she had made the journey in only sixty-eight days.

As they drifted past the quay that held the *Marco Polo*, the mate suddenly gave an order. "Canso, stand by to throw the rope ashore. John, José, Santana, stand by to cast off the towrope." Docking the square-rigger took a series of well-coordinated actions, and the crew would have to look sharp.

Canso stood on the foredeck, a heavy coil of rope used to moor the ship at his feet, and a length of light half-inch rope tied to it. At one end of the light rope was a knotted ball which the sailor twirled around his head. The tug had pulled them close to the Queen's docks, and as they drifted past the wharf, Canso threw the light rope twenty feet to a man standing on shore. When he caught it, the longshoreman pulled the heavy rope ashore and looped it over the big iron stanchion that was on the dock.

As soon as the rope was ashore, the mate signalled the tug. The steam-driven vessel reversed her propeller; the towrope went slack and fell into the water. "Cast off the towrope," the mate ordered, and the next moment it was thrown over the bow and the *Scotian* drifted free of the tug.

A moment later the heavy rope to the wharf became taut. The ship hesitated and then its stem began swinging around with the momentum. “All hands man the capstan,” was the mate’s order and he looped the heavy rope over the drum. The sailors fitted in the capstan bars and slowly began winching the ship toward the wharf.

Tommy began the chorus of the capstan shanty, *Liverpool Ladies*, and the sailors joined in as they slowly pushed their capstan bars. There was an atmosphere of expectancy among the crew. For the first time in weeks they would be going ashore.

It took two hours of winching, but finally the ship was into the pool, away from the fast currents of the harbour, and the gates were closed behind them. By the time they were docked, fog had swept in from the Irish Sea and a cold, drizzling rain had begun. The men shivered as they worked.

As soon as they touched the wharf, the captain went ashore, leaving orders that they were to begin rigging up the winches for unloading cane as soon as they were tied up. The crew were tired, wet and frozen, but they went below to put on their oilskins. Then they began slowly rigging up the boom on the mainmast. They were grateful when it was too dark to work and could go in for supper.

Afterwards, the crew, along with Meg and Mr. Pepper, gathered in the forecastle. John and Meg huddled near the lantern and began writing a letter home in the hope that a fast steamer to New York would get it there before they arrived. The sailors’ anticipation rose. They had been cooped up for so long under the tight discipline of the officers that they were impatient to be given permission to go ashore. As they played cards, a tone of bitterness and frustration gradually crept into their conversation.

"I can see myself goin' down the main street with a skin full of rum and a lady on each arm," said Tommy wistfully.

"Aye, you can see it but can you get yerself ashore with money in yer pocket from this passage?" said Mr. Pepper. "The cap'n's not known to be the sailor's friend."

"He'd better if he knows what's good for him," said the seaman with sudden determination.

"What would you do?" asked John.

"I'd get him some way, be sure of that. He'd have to be watchin' all the time ...."

Just at that moment the captain, mate and bosun burst into the crowded quarters. The crew immediately stopped what they had been doing. Captain Barnard stood near the candle lantern. The light flickered in his face showing the strain in his blue eyes.

He started awkwardly. "We made it from Jamaica in good time, but we're not to be in Liverpool for long. What I've come to say is that there'll be no leave for any crewman. You'll be paid off when we get back to Canada and not before. There'll be no drunken seamen in my crew and I won't have any man deserting. Is that understood? Tomorrow we'll be unloading cane at daybreak and the sooner we get out of this port the better off we'll be."

For a moment no one in the crew could find anything to say. They had looked forward so much to shore leave, planning what taverns they would visit and the things they would do.

Tommy was the first to react. "Cap'n, that's not fair. We've worked hard and we need time off. You can't hold us here as if we're prisoners." He was on his feet along with Scobie, Georges and others.

"I'll not have any of my crew deserting!"

John was beside Tommy. "It's not fair captain. We need time ashore."

The captain's face darkened. "You men listen and listen well to what I say. Every crew member aboard this ship is guilty of mutiny. Mutiny, do you hear!" he shouted. "You stopped me from flogging Canso. You disobeyed a direct order. All I need to do is report you to the British Admiralty and you could be hung for your crime. Do you understand?" He shouted it out, his anger finally getting the better of him. "Unless you want that to happen you'll follow my orders. There will be no shore leave and that's the end of it!"

The seamen watched their master warily, wondering if his threats were real, but not one of them was willing to take a chance and defy him. Suddenly the captain turned and left, followed by his two officers.

"Damn his soul!" Tommy cursed at the closed door. The young British seaman kicked the table in anger and swore under his breath. "I tell you we'll rot in this ship. Rot, I tell you!" Others murmured agreement. "We should desert this floating hell. Let the cap'n sail this tub back to Canada himself."

"That's right," said others. "Let's all do it ,Tommy," said Scobie.

"What do you think, Canso?" asked José.

The big Nova Scotian seaman had said nothing through the whole confrontation. Now he shifted uncomfortably because he knew the others looked to him for leadership.

"We can do nothing," he said softly.

"What do you mean?"

"You know Liverpool always has seamen looking for a berth. If we deserted, the cap'n could get a crew in a day and not even have to use a crimp. What with the Depression, there'll be a crowd of sailors on the beach. All that would happen is that we would lose our wages. We'd be without work."

No one said a word. They all knew that Canso was right, but that did not help their bitter feelings toward the captain.

"Well, I say that we should be given at least one night on the town," said Tommy.

The others seemed to be considering the alternatives. Either they stay aboard and accept the captain's orders or go ashore and spend weeks or maybe months unemployed without a penny for support. There was nothing to do but resign themselves to their fate. Slowly they turned back to their card games and conversation.

Meg, John and Canso were sitting on a bunk together. "Tommy's right," said Meg quietly so the others would not hear. "We should be given time off so we can go into the city. We've worked hard enough for the cap'n. That's the least he should do."

"That's right," said John. "And using that threat about the mutiny is not fair. That happened a long time ago. What do you think, Canso?"

"The captain's the officer," Canso said, avoiding their gaze. "We're not paid to think."

"What do you mean?" said John, alarmed at his friend's gloomy mood. "We've got our rights, don't we?"

Canso only shrugged his shoulders, got up and walked over to the low door of the forecastle. He lit up his small sailor's clay pipe and did not turn around when John came up beside him.

"What's wrong, Canso?" John asked. "Why are you on the captain's side now?"

"He's in command, John. He'll always be in command." Canso sighed, breathing out a puff of bitter smoke. "And he's right about the mutiny. He's got the law on his side."

"But we won, Canso."

"There's no victory in it, John. Aye, I'm thankful not to be flogged, but what else did we win? The ship's the same. The hull still leaks, the crew is overworked and underpaid. A mere sailor never wins." With a restless gesture, he knocked his pipe against the side of the door and put it back in his pocket. "Don't listen to me John, it's just that I'm starting to wonder about my life. Fifteen years a sailor, and still I have nothing."

"You do, though," John said, disturbed at Canso's obvious misery. "You've got your health, and good friends, and a job you know how to do."

Canso smiled wearily and clapped a heavy hand on John's shoulder. "Friends I have, but will I see them again after this voyage? Health is a frail thing. I'm not a young man anymore, John, after fifteen years on the ocean. Well, but never mind me."

Then, before the boy could say anything, Canso had gone out alone on deck. Meg came up to John, an anxious look on her face.

"What's wrong with him?" she asked. "He's changed so much."

"It's all right," John said, uncertainly. "We'll just have to find some way to cheer him up."

The next morning the captain was sitting with the mate and bosun when Meg came in from the galley to serve them. He seemed to be studying her for a long time and then said, "I'll be going to the city today, Meg. If you like, I'll take you with me so you can see something of the city."

Meg was surprised and even a trifle suspicious. She had never seen the captain make an offer like this, but then she was anxious to see the city. "I'd like that. Thank you."

"Good," he went back to his breakfast, but as if in an afterthought he said, "But you'll be putting on your dress and leaving those terrible sailors' clothes behind."

"Yes, sir." Meg smiled to think that her outfit still annoyed the captain. She was about to leave the officers' dining room when she paused. "Ah, do you think that we could bring along my brother John, sir?"

The captain looked up at her warily. "He's been a troublemaker, that one."

"But he's worked hard sir, and he deserves a chance to see the city."

"No, one of you Bains children is enough for me. And I want no high jinks from the likes of you, understand."

Meg started to object, and then she realized that the captain was smiling at her. His bluff manner was hiding the fact that he liked Meg, and, in fact, depended on her as his only friend aboard ship. She smiled back, and went off to dress in her best long yellow cotton dress. An hour later she was climbing over the side of the ship and running down the wharf in search of a cab for her and the captain.

It was not long past dawn but already the streets were crowded. Teamsters were hauling loads from the big stone warehouses to the waiting ships and from the ships back to the warehouses. There were people of all types and descriptions jamming the streets.

Finally, after running through back alleys and streets, Meg hailed a hansom cab. She was very excited as she climbed aboard the two-wheeled covered carriage. The driver, wearing a sober dark grey morning coat and top hat, sat behind her in an elevated seat. The dapple-grey horse trotted along the cobble-stoned streets with its iron-shod hooves clopping on the pavement, and Meg sat proudly in the cab feeling very self-important.

When they got back to the ship, she scrambled aboard to fetch the captain. Already the crew had taken off the hatches and were winching up the sugar cane, and swinging it over the side to waiting wagons. She felt guilty that she was not doing her share of the chores, but when Santana smiled and waved she knew the crew were pleased that she, at least, had an opportunity for a tour of the city.

The captain gave the driver an address, squeezed in beside her and they were off. The two of them studied the people they passed with fascination. There were merchant sailors dressed sloppily in rough woollen coats and peaked caps, groups of British naval seamen in dark blue middies and white pants, longshoremen carrying their loading hooks over their shoulders and prosperous-looking businessmen dressed in morning coats. But more than any other group were the hundreds of shabbily dressed men and women who had come to Liverpool looking for a cheap passage to the New World.

At first they drove down narrow lanes past high stone warehouses until they came to a district filled with drinking establishments and cheap hotels. This merged into an area more prosperous than the others, the business district of ship provisioners and shipping agents. The cab driver reigned in his horses and they stopped in front of one of the business entrances.

Captain Barnard got out first and Meg followed. After the cab driver was paid off, they entered the building. The place comprised a series of small offices leading off a central hallway. They scanned the writing on the doors until Meg found one saying: *William Becker, Esquire, Passenger Broker*. The captain knocked loudly, and on hearing a response from inside, turned the handle.

It was a large, high-ceilinged room with a bay window overlooking a courtyard. In one corner a coal fire burned to take the chill off the air and Indian rugs were scattered on the dark floor. A large walnut desk stood in front of the window and behind it sat a big heavy man dressed in a prosperous dark suit and waist-coat. His face was pallid, his fair hair receding.

"Yes?" the man said, barely looking up from his newspaper.

The captain seemed rough and unkempt by comparison. "Ah, I'm Cap'n Barnard," he began awkwardly. "I'm from the ship *Scotian*. We're just in from Jamaica with a load of sugar cane and I'd like to ship out to Halifax, Canada, as soon as possible. I was told that you arrange passengers and I was wondering if ...." The captain's voice trailed off.

The broker was leaning across his desk staring intently at the captain and the young girl beside him. "You were wondering if I could get you some steerage emigrants so you could head back home with a paying cargo," he said, completing the captain's thought.

"Yes, that's right." The broker got to his feet. He was an enormous man, well over six feet tall and he carried a fat belly in front. He felt in his waistcoat pocket and brought out a long cheroot, struck a sulphur match and puffed on the cigar until his head was wreathed in smoke.

"Won't you sit down, Cap'n?" He motioned to one of the two leather seats in front of the desk.

Captain Barnard hesitated awkwardly but then accepted the invitation. He nudged Meg who perched uncomfortably in the other seat. The big broker puffed thoughtfully on his cheroot, and then set his heavy bulk on the side of the desk. "So you want me to find you some passengers?" He spoke with a thick Liverpool working-class accent.

"Yes, that's right."

"Tell me about yer ship and yer plans, Cap'n?"

The *Scotian's* a three-masted ship of 960 tons, made out of Nova Scotian pine," the captain said proudly. "She was built first for the California and Australian runs, but now, with the hard times for the windships, she was converted to a timber drogher. But she still has the speed of the clipper in her."

The passenger broker studied his cigar. "She's a wooden-hulled windjammer, Cap'n," he sighed. "Problems with them, you know. Most of the emigrants have been taken over to America in the steam-driven iron ships for the past, oh, twenty-odd years now. Not many willin' to risk it in the windjammers 'cause they say it's unsafe and things like that. Still, a few sailing ships that go out do take passengers."

"What if we charged less for the passage than the steamers? Do you think we could fill the ship?"

"Well, maybe, Cap'n. Maybe. But then I don't know. There's the emigration agent to worry about 'n' everything."

"But she's a clipper," said the captain anxiously. "We could make the passage to Halifax in three weeks. What with the winter winds and all we might do it faster than some of the steamer runs."

The broker studied his cigar. A slight smile came over his face. "What was the charge that you've been thinkin' of, Cap'n?"

"Well, I don't know, something less than the charge of the steamers."

"Mmm. Their prices are somewhere around eight pounds. Now if you were to charge something like half that. Let's say four pound ten, we may be able to fill the hold for you."

"That would be good, Mr. Becker."

"Things are tough in these parts since the Depression started earlier this year. Men are out of work by the thousands in the cotton mills here in Lancashire, and in the coal mines they say the unemployment is terrible. Every day the trains bring crowds of men here to Liverpool looking for work. You'll see them there on the streets traipsing about with their carpetbags. Pathetic it is 'cause there's not work in these parts. There's no work anywhere in the British Isles."

The broker folded his arms around his generous stomach. "Now there is North America. In these parts people think of Canada as a country flowin' with milk and honey." He smiled at the thought of it. "What we'd be doin' is offerin' them hope, Cap'n. We'd give 'em a cheap passage and in three weeks they'd be in Canada where they could get jobs and everythin'. We'd be offerin' them a service, wouldn't we?"

Meg could not keep silent. "But they'll just go to unemployment in Canada." The captain and passenger broker looked at the girl for a brief moment and then ignored the comment.

"Yes, that's right, Mr. Becker, we'd be offering them a service," said the captain.

The big man drew heavily on his cheroot and exhaled the smoke in a long thin stream. "Now Cap'n. It seems that we are agreed. We will have to do a little selling and maybe try to deal with the emigration agents in some way, if you know what I mean. You leave the details to me. The only thing left to agree on is money." He paused for a moment avoiding the stares of the captain and his young associate by studying his cheroot. "Let us say that you fill your hold with passengers, Cap'n, and I'll take twenty percent of the cost of the ticket."

The captain was amazed. "Twenty percent!"

"That's right, Cap'n. You see this is going to be a little more difficult to arrange. There's the emigration agent who will have to … ah … be taken care of. Then I'll have to do a lot of sellin'. You must know the difficulties, Cap'n."

Captain Barnard was suddenly decisive. He stood to his feet. "Twenty percent is robbery. That's almost one pound per person. You'll be making most of the profit."

Mr. Becker stood up, his stomach swelling in front of him. "By all means, Cap'n. But you'll find that I'm the only broker that can help you in Liverpool. Obviously that's why they referred you to me."

"What do you mean?"

"It's just that … well, you understand. Most sailing ships do not have an easy time passing the emigration agent's requirements, and you see I … well, let us say I have learned to deal with these difficulties."

The captain paused. He looked to Meg as if trying to find help in deciding what to do. "You mean … " he began but then stopped. The broker had made himself very clear. The two men stared at each other for what seemed to be a long time. Mr. Becker had a slight smile on his face and the captain seemed stunned. Then slowly the captain returned to his seat with a look of utter resignation.

"You are wise, Cap'n," said the broker with a smile. "A cargo is very difficult to get in these hard times. Now, just to complete the details."

The big man went behind his desk, took a clean sheet of paper, dipped his pen in the ink well and readied himself for writing. "Now, Cap'n. Your destination?"

"Halifax, Nova Scotia."

The broker carefully copied it down.

"And what will be your sailing date?"

"Three weeks from today. December 10th, 1873."

CHAPTER 11

WHEN they got back on the street, the captain could no longer contain himself. "I did it!" he said excitedly. "We've got a cargo. Now the ship's going to be mine. All mine."

They began walking back in the direction of the ship with the captain explaining as they went. "You see, I owe money for the *Scotian*. I had to borrow from the bank, and they've been trying to get it back. More than once I had to set to sea before they repossessed the ship. Then my luck began to turn. I got the cargo of timber to Jamaica, then the sugar cane to Liverpool, and now we'll have passengers for the 'tween decks to pay the voyage home."

His eyes brightened as he lost himself in fantasy. "When I get to Halifax, I'll have the money for the bank. Think of that. I'll take the money to the banker, and I'll lay it out on his desk for him to see. I'll pile it up in great stacks and then the *Scotian* will be mine."

The master paused in the middle of the street, lost in his own daydream. "I'll be the cap'n of my own ship. I can go anywhere in the world … take voyages where no man works hard. I'll be free."

Meg was suddenly angry. "So it's true that you work us so hard because you're afraid of losing the ship."

"You don't understand," the captain said.

"You just want to get back to Halifax with your money. You don't care about your crew or passengers or anybody."

"That'll be enough from you, young lady," blustered the captain. If it had been one of his sailors, he would have shouted or delivered a hard clout to the ear, but with Meg he clearly was at a loss. "I thought you were on my side."

"There aren't any sides. I don't care about your problems. I am only concerned about what you are doing to your ship and your crew." As the captain stood there open-mouthed, Meg almost felt sorry for him, but her sense of injustice had been sparked. "I like you and I think you mean no harm, but the way you treat other people is a disgrace."

"You're a child," snapped the man. "It's my ship."

"No, it's our ship. We run it." Meg was almost breathless with rage. Suddenly she stamped her foot. "Run it yourself if you think you can. You'd have a fine time sailing it by yourself. You're nothing but a greedy old fool!"

With that she turned on her heel and hurried away down the cobblestones, leaving the captain sputtering with anger on the empty street. But as Meg ran on, her emotions began to cool. Name-calling would do no good if she wanted to make the captain listen to reason. She would have to control her temper if she ever wanted people to stop thinking of her as a child. Sadly, she climbed back aboard the *Scotian*, the joy and expectation of that morning completely gone.

A grey, icy mist had descended over the ship, and Meg watched glumly as the crew began unloading the big bundles of sugar cane over the side. Santana and José operated the hand winch which raised the cane out of the hold and swung them over the side, Tommy and Hans unloaded them into the backs of horse-drawn wagons and the rest of the crew worked in the hold.

The huge bundles were very awkward. They had to be worked free and then rolled across the layer of cane so they could be winched out through the main hatch. Often it was only Canso's enormous strength that could get the huge bundles into position. More than once the crew members were cut by the sharp ends of the cane or stumbled as their foot slipped into a hole.

When the captain came back on board that afternoon he went straight to the hold to see how the work was progressing. He was careful not to look at Meg, but she could tell that his earlier excitement was gone and his restless anxiety about his ship had returned. The master complained that the crew were not working fast enough and when he went back on deck the men cursed him.

After the evening meal the crew collected in the forecastle. Meg related what had happened on the trip to the city. Curiously, the men had little interest in the captain's financial problems. Most of them had suspected that or even worse, but they were all concerned with the news that they would be shipping out to Halifax in three weeks' time, the hold filled with emigrants.

It was Canso who was most upset. "He can't do that. This ship's in no condition to carry passengers."

"Shouldn't be allowed," said Scobie, and the others sitting on their bunks in the dim candlelight nodded agreement.

"We've got to do something about it, Canso," said John.

"We've got to stop him before something bad happens," added Meg.

"But what can we do?" Deep lines of worry marked Canso's face. "We have no power. We can do nothing."

"We can send a delegation to the cap'n," said John. "And tell him that he should get another cargo."

"That won't do anything. He'll just take on another crew and we'll be left on the beach."

"But Canso, we can't let him take on passengers if it's dangerous," said Meg intently. "It wouldn't be fair."

"Fair! Fair! What is fair about this voyage!" Canso shouted angrily. "What is fair about anything we do?"

John was furious. "Canso, you won't do anything. Once you fought against the cap'n for what was right — you stood up to him — but now you do nothing."

The big seaman looked desperate. "The cap'n is a driven man and he'll stop at nothing to get a paying cargo to Halifax. Don't you see that?"

"All I understand, Canso, is that you've given up," said John. "You do nothing to help us."

"But …." Canso gave up his explanation before he started. He turned away, hurt that the boy would think so badly of him. How could he explain that their ideas meant nothing to the captain? There was not a thing that would stop him from taking a paying cargo to Halifax, and if they were to try, it was likely the captain would charge them with mutiny this time.

For a long time the forecastle was quiet. The small lantern flickering by the doorway cast an eerie light over the faces of the crew. No one stirred: Canso would not take the leadership and the others lacked the confidence to do anything on their own. Finally Mr. Pepper got to his feet. "Come on Meg, we all need some sleep. These next three weeks will see some hard work."

The unloading of the cane was a dirty, backbreaking job. The crew was up before dawn and spent the whole day and part of the night rolling the big bundles of cane over to the hatch, winching them up, and hauling them over to the wagons at the quay side. Finally, when they finished five days later, they were tired and sore from cuts and scrapes, but the captain gave them no more than half a day's rest. At the afternoon high tide, the gates of the pool were opened; they winched the *Scotian* out into the harbour and a tug towed them across to the Birkenhead side of the Mersey.

They dropped anchor at the ballast pile and began loading rock. It was terrible work. The weather had turned worse. Wind and rain drove in from the Irish Sea and the cold kept the men constantly shivering and their hands numb. They wore their oilskins all day but still they could not keep out the damp and the cold.

The captain seemed worse than ever, keeping to himself, talking to no one. But he watched his crew closely, as if hoping to catch one of the hands doing something wrong. Often John would see him restlessly pacing the deck with a grim look on his face, and the boy wondered what tormented him so.

The ballast pile was rough and steep. The men had to climb over sharp rocks that were slippery from the rain. Their fingers tore as they worked to get the boulders free and roll them down to the slings that were used to hoist them aboard. By the end of the third day they were so exhausted they barely had the strength to eat their supper, but at last the mate announced that they were finished.

The next morning they raised anchor and a steam tug towed them to the Waterloo docks on the Liverpool side of the harbour. Once inside the pool, they brought three wagonloads of lumber into the hold to build the between-deck. This would be the living quarters for the passengers.

While the sailors laboured to prepare the ship for the voyage, Meg and Mr. Pepper were responsible for ordering and storing all of the provisions. This was a complicated task at the best of times, but it was not made any easier by having a captain as exacting as the master of the *Scotian*.

In many of the early voyages to North America, passengers had to provide their own food but now regulations made this the responsibility of the ship's owner. Mr. Pepper started his calculations for how much food they would need on the basis of a four-week crossing, but the captain insisted that they could easily make Halifax in three weeks and the cook had to considerably revise his shopping list.

Water was one of the most important commodities aboard an emigrant ship. Many a crossing of the Atlantic had been made with water that had been pure at the start but filthy and disease-laden in the end. The regulations called for three quarts of water per adult per day. Mr. Pepper ordered twenty three-hundred-gallon tanks, or sweet casks as they were called, and when they arrived had them installed on the main deck.

The food was the most difficult thing to order, but after talking with the captain Mr. Pepper's shortened list included barrels of salt beef and pork, flour, hardtack biscuits, oatmeal, potatoes, a little molasses and a small quantity of rice. If there was to be other variety in their diet, the passengers would have to supply it themselves.

The task of preparing the between-decks was organized by the bosun. The work was mainly inside the ship, out of the cold winter wind and rain, but the captain still hounded them in an attempt to keep to the December 10th sailing date. The steerage compartment was about one hundred and twenty-five feet long — the length of the ship — and twenty-five feet wide. First a rough floor had to be laid across the beams, above the ballast, to make the compartment. This left a little more than six feet of head room, but most people had to crouch in order to avoid hitting the numerous beams that dropped another four inches.

On each side of the compartment, running the whole length of the ship, they built bunks about five and a half feet long and six feet wide, made out of rough lumber. Each berth could accommodate six adults or a family of ten. In front of the bunks were aisles, and then, running the whole length of the ship, the crew built one long table with benches on either side.

One day when the work was close to completion, John was talking to the bosun and mentioned how cramped the quarters seemed to be. The old seaman smiled. "You think these conditions are bad? Let me tell you lad, when I was a young seaman your age, running the passage between Liverpool and Québec, many of the timber droghers were full to the scuppers with emigrants. The cap'n would pack them in by the hundreds. They'd get sick and the cholera would spread among them, and we'd run out of food, and the water would turn sour. Those were terrible voyages. Nightmares. By comparison, this'll be like a holiday."

But the boy found it hard to think of conditions being worse than living at sea in the between-decks of the *Scotian*. The closer they got to the sailing date, the more people would come down to look at the ship. Some insisted on coming aboard for an inspection. Many of them went away in disgust, swearing that people should not be subjected to such conditions, but many others went away silently, knowing that no matter what the conditions, they had little choice but to make the voyage.

Less than a week remained before sailing when Meg went ashore with Mr. Pepper for added provisions and returned with a poster she found which advertised the sailing of the ship. That night the crew huddled around the candle to see it. Many of the men could not read English, so John read it aloud.

"The fast clipper ship *Scotian* is sailing for Halifax, Nova Scotia on December 10, 1873. The crossing will take three weeks or less. Canada offers abundant employment for all trades. Price four pounds ten. Children under 14 half-price, babes-in-arms free. Meals included."

"Four pounds ten," scoffed Tommy. "That's robbery for a ship like this."

"Those people will live like animals down in the hold," said Georges.

José was more disgusted than any of the rest. "We do nothing. I am sick of it. We work to complete the steerage. We see how bad things will be. What can we do, Canso?"

But the man they had always looked to for leadership could not even face his mates. "We can do nothing," Canso said softly. "Nothing." Then he turned and left the forecastle.

"I tell you he's not one of us any more," said John. "He does nothing but back the cap'n all the time."

"Stop it, John," Meg shot back. "He's just upset. That's all."

The next few days the crew rushed to finish the steerage compartment in preparation for the voyage. Extra hatches were cut for ventilation, plate racks were made under the table, places were built for storing trunks, and two open fireplaces were made on the foredeck in large wooden cases lined with bricks.

The passengers began to arrive a week before their embarkation date. They would come aboard, show the mate their ticket, stow their baggage on the ship and then go back out onto the quay. Those who could not afford a cheap hotel room built fires on the waterfront and slept in the cold wet air with little protection save an old blanket. At night the sailors could stand on deck and see their numerous fires; they knew that the emigrants were anxiously waiting for the voyage to begin.

Two days before sailing, the emigration agent arrived for an inspection. He was elegantly dressed for a government employee. Rather than dirty his new outfit on deck, he went straight to the captain's quarters. A little longer than an hour later, the captain escorted the agent to the gangway and the inspection was completed.

The night before they were to set sail, the crew found time for their own celebration. After supper they gathered in the forecastle, and once inside, Tommy bolted the door. He went back to his bunk and pulled out two bottles of rum. "Even if the cap'n won't let us have shore leave, we're going to have a good time."

The sailors were happy at the sight of the liquor and they congratulated Tommy good-humouredly on his resourcefulness. They quickly found ways of pulling the corks out of the bottles and began passing them from man to man. Each seaman took a quick drink and then passed the bottle on to the next.

When the bottle came to John and Meg they both passed it on without taking a drink, but the sailors would not accept that. "Come on, boy. You're a seaman now. You've got to have a drink," Tommy insisted. The others joined in until there was nothing John could do other than to taste the rum.

He put the bottle to his lips and took a swig. "Phew! It's awful!" and he spit out the foul-tasting stuff. The crew laughed as if it had been a great joke.

The crew were in high spirits until the hostility between Canso and Tommy broke out in earnest. Both men had been drinking heavily but Tommy seemed particularly drunk. He had been deriding the conditions aboard ship when suddenly he turned on Canso. "There's your man who loves the cap'n," he said drunkenly.

Canso did not move.

"It's true, isn't it? You support the cap'n all the time. Did he pay you to keep an eye on us, Canso? Did he?"

"Stop it, Tommy!" Canso was angry.

"You're on his side, ain't you? You do your work and you don't say nothin'."

"I'm warning you. I won't put up with this."

"Yer 'fraid of him. That's it. 'Fraid of him." Tommy was on his feet as if he was going to do something. He weaved unsteadily. "That's right, isn't it, Canso? Yer 'fraid of him! "I'll do you in before you get us!" He lurched in Canso's direction.

Canso stood up, towering over Tommy. He brought his hand back as if he was going to strike. Tommy cowered, instinctively. It seemed that they stood like that for a long time before Canso broke the silence:

"Damn it!" he said harshly. "We've turned into brutes."

A moment later he slid back the bolt of the door and disappeared into the drizzling cold rain on deck.

CHAPTER 12

AT dawn there was a break in the wet, cold, overcast weather. The sun shone between broken clouds, drying the puddles and warming the quay where the *Scotian* was moored.

The emigrants poured onto the wharf by the hundreds, anxious to get settled aboard the ship. There were women, children and men all awkwardly carrying parcels of every shape and description. But when they tried to go up the gangway, the bosun blocked their way and announced that boarding would begin at ten o'clock. The people settled down on their packages, content to wait.

The crew could not help but share the excitement of the passengers. When the mate rigged up the pump and his watch began their monotonous chore, they talked and laughed good-naturedly. There was much running of messages and scrambling up the rigging to see that everything was in good order. As they performed their chores, the sailors were conscious that there were over three hundred pairs of eyes watching their every movement.

About nine in the morning Meg was on deck when she recognized the passenger broker making his way through the crowd. He was with two other younger men in their early twenties who carried suitcases. All three were well dressed, but the broker's huge bulk was immaculately tailored in a morning coat, striped trousers and top hat. In his right hand he carried a gold-headed cane as if for protection against the roughly dressed people who surrounded him. The three men weaved their way through the tightly thronged emigrants, forced their way up the gangway and identified themselves to the bosun. They were ushered immediately to the captain's quarters.

It was nearing ten o'clock when the captain emerged with his visitors. They walked to the gangway where Mr. Becker, the broker, offered the captain a gloved hand. "I hope our arrangements work well Cap'n," the crew overheard him say. "Maybe we'll have more business of this kind in the future." He left with a flourish, using his walking cane to open a way through the crowd for him.

The captain stood at the main deck rail surveying the milling crowd on the quay. As he turned, John and the others could see that his face was grim, as if he was not looking forward to the passage. "Stow the pump handles," he ordered suddenly. The crew moved quickly. They knew the captain would insist that they look sharp.

He looked back at the crowd. "Are we ready to take the passengers aboard, Mr. Ryerson?"

"Aye, sir."

"This is Mr. Burns, who will be the clerk for the voyage, and Dr. Fraser, the physician. They'll help keep order."

"Aye, sir." The bosun shook hands with the new additions to the officers' ranks.

"There's three hundred and sixty passengers altogether. Try and get a view of their tickets as they come aboard. Let them go below and find a berth and then tell them to assemble above deck. Carry on, Mr. Ryerson." And then the captain headed back to his quarters.

The passengers were all on their feet now, sensing that something was about to happen. "Show your tickets as you board!" the bosun shouted above the din. The crowd of people pressed forward, laughing and talking to each other as they made their way aboard ship.

John and Meg scrambled up on the poop deck and leaned over the rail to watch the scene. Most of the people were English workers drawn from the north country. The Depression had hit the English industrial towns and cities particularly hard, creating massive unemployment. These people had gathered together the last of their resources to make the move to the New World in the hopes of finding a better life.

The majority of the passengers were young men and women in their twenties and early thirties. There were weavers and spinners from Lancashire, coal miners from Yorkshire and the Midlands, and every kind of mechanic and engineer. Most were without any specific kind of trade but had laboured at a variety of different types of manual work.

As well as the English workers there were many Irish families in the crowd. They could be easily picked out. Most were farm labourers dressed in ragged, warm clothing. Less than thirty years before, the potato famine had cut the Irish population to a quarter of its number but still the people fled, trying to escape absentee landlords and oppressive taxes.

There were not only young single people, but also many married couples with children. There were infants in arms, and children by the score played at their parents' feet as they waited to board the ship. There were even a few older people still strong enough to pull up stakes and move thousands of miles from home looking for a better life.

Of the scores of emigrants, most had said their goodbyes in their home villages and had walked or taken carriages or trains to Liverpool, but some had relatives at the quay to see them off on their long voyage. People were crying uncontrollably, clinging together in the sorrow of anticipated separation. For most it would be years before they ever saw their relatives again and for some the separation would be permanent.

Meg and John could not help but be touched by the scene. These people were leaving everything that they knew in the hopes of a better life across the Atlantic. But what if things turned out badly? What if conditions in Canada were worse than anything they had experienced at home? What would happen to them then?

Slowly the passengers filed on board ship and went below to find a berth. The mate, Mr. Mckenzie, provided some type of rough organization by directing the young single men to the forward part of the compartment and the single women to the aft section. The rest was random. Individuals or families would choose a bunk, place their belongings on it to indicate that it had been taken, and then go back on deck to mingle with the crowd.

Despite the crowded milling-about, there was a happy sense of expectation aboard the *Scotian*. People introduced themselves and the single women, outfitted in their full dresses and sun hats, were the centres of attention for the young men. The passengers helped each other carry heavy trunks, and whenever an older couple came aboard, there were always extra hands to help them down the hatchway and carry their belongings.

The children were having the best time of all. Quickly they made friends, and ran up and down the narrow passageways in the steerage quarters or scrambled all over the upper deck. More than once, sailors caught the more daring boys beginning to climb up the shrouds and gave them a lecture about the dangers aloft.

Mr. Pepper knew that people would be hungry so he had prepared two big vats of beef broth soup over the open fireplaces early in the morning. At noon the crew were ordered to serve the lunch. It turned into a party of sorts, with plenty of good humour and the opportunity to make new friends.

Finally at one o'clock the captain appeared on the poop deck and shouted, "All ashore who's going ashore!"

The bosun picked up the order and climbed into the steerage compartment. "All ashore who's going ashore!" he repeated several times and then climbed up on deck to shout the command several times again.

The friends and relatives of the passengers said their last farewells and left the ship. The fires on the foredeck were extinguished and the pots taken away.

"Stand by," shouted the captain and the crew members hurried to their posts near the lines. Slowly the gate to the pool was opened by the harbour master.

"Cast off aft lincs!" The captain shouted at the top of his voice so he could be heard above the din of the crowd. When they were aboard, he shouted, "Cast off forward lines!" A rope led from the capstan on the ship to a stanchion on the wharf outside the pool. With the order of "Man the capstan" all the crew members began pushing on their capstan bars to winch the ship forward and out through the gates of the pool. Once they were out, the ship had to be turned at right angles and winched down another narrow channel until they were in the Mersey River. The waiting steam tug tossed a line to the *Scotian* and they were under tow.

The people who were at the quay saying their goodbyes had rushed to another part of the wharf to get a better view. As the tug fastened its line to the ship, they suddenly let out a cheer and waved their hats in the air. The emigrants lining the rail of the *Scotian* cheered at the tops of their voices in reply. Slowly the ship gained momentum and the wharf began slipping behind. There was a scramble for the aft section of the ship so that the passengers could get a last glimpse of their friends and relatives. Some men even climbed a few feet up the mizzen shrouds, waving their hats in the air until those on the wharf were small indistinguishable figures.

"All passengers assemble on the fore and main decks," shouted the bosun in his loudest voice. He repeated himself several times and then went into the steerage compartment to repeat the order.

When everyone was assembled the captain stood at the poop rail and addressed the passengers. "I am Cap'n Barnard, the master of the *Scotian*," he shouted in a voice loud enough to be heard above the wind and commotion. "We're outward bound for Halifax. The clerk here, Mr. Burns, will be reading the passenger's list and any who do not hold a ticket will be put on the steam tug before we cast off the towline. I want to say that there'll be rules aboard my ship, and they'll be followed to the letter. Anyone who breaks them will have trouble with me. I will appoint a committee of four men to be your spokesmen and to enforce the rules. One further thing. I won't have you interfering with my crew. When you're above deck, keep to yourselves. That is all."

The captain concluded his speech as abruptly as it had begun. He then turned the proceedings over to Mr. Burns, a slight fellow with delicate hands and arms. He began calling out names on the passengers' list. As each name was called, the person or family would go to the bosun or doctor to have their ticket checked. Then they would stand in a special roped-off section of the ship.

While this was going on, the mate took the crew members on a thorough search of the ship looking for stowaways. They went through the steerage compartment, looking through the stacks of trunks and carpetbags. Then they went to the various storage areas on the ship and probed among the barrels, sacks of flour and rolls of sailcloth. The mate even sent a group of sailors into the forecastle. Stowaways were a common occurrence on ships travelling to North America. The misery of many people was so great that they were willing to suffer any amount of hardship to find escape, but the sailors found none aboard the *Scotian*.

After the tedious chore of reading the passengers' list, the only fraud that was found was that of an Irish couple who had represented their seventeen-year-old son as being under fourteen. The couple and the boy were taken before the captain by Mr. Burns, who gave an elaborate explanation.

"You'll either have to pay the two pounds five or the boy will be put aboard the tug," Captain Barnard announced curtly.

"But, sir, we don't have the money," the woman pleaded. "You can't take the boy from us," and she burst into tears.

A number of passengers had overheard the conversation. Within a few minutes a collection had been taken up and the extra fare was paid to the captain. The Irish couple were so happy that they thanked the people over and over again for their generosity.

The roll call and search for stowaways had taken an hour and a half. By the time they were finished, the city of Liverpool was fast fading from view, and they were well into the broad Mersey estuary. In spite of the cold, most of the people stayed on deck watching their country fade from view.

There was a holiday feeling in the air now. Someone brought out a fiddle, and another a flute and bagpipes. Before long, one of the young Yorkshire workers had organized four-handed jigs and reels on the main deck. The women talked as they sat near the rail, and the children played or sang along with the tunes.

With the exception of the occasional sigh or tear, it was apparent that there was little despair in leaving the British Isles. Many passengers had spent a lifetime under the rule of absentee landlords or tyrannical mill bosses and some had spent years in unemployment and poverty. They were expecting a new and better life in Canada. A new future lay before them, and the memory of misery was all that was left behind.

Most of the crew were on the foredeck, awaiting the order to cast off the line to the tug and set sails. Meg had been there since lunch talking to passengers and enjoying the sun. Canso and John joined her and the three slouched against the rail watching the dancing and the fun.

For some reason it put them all in a pensive mood. Seeing so many families and children reminded John and Meg of their own family in Ottawa and they repeated their concern that their mother would be having a difficult time.

Canso listened quietly to the talk before joining in. "It seems strange to be going back to Nova Scotia. I've not been home in such a long time."

"Why don't you visit your family when we get there, Canso?" asked Meg.

The big sailor seemed lost in thought for a moment. "I don't know," he said quietly. "Maybe I could. It's not too far from Halifax, but it's been so long now."

"Are you afraid to go?"

"No, it's not that." He was quiet for a moment. "When I look at these men with their families ... their wives and children ... I see that they have so much and I have so little ...."

"But Canso, you don't even try to change your life," said Meg. "You could have tried to stand up to the captain before. Every member of the crew would have followed you."

Canso only shook his head, and Meg felt her temper begin to flare up. But this time, she controlled it with an effort, and said, very softly, "Nothing good will happen unless you do something yourself. Look at how happy those emigrants are down there, laughing and dancing. The future is uncertain for them, but at least they are trying to change for the better in a new country."

Canso nodded slowly, as if beginning to think things through. Then he smiled at her, and Meg watched as he moved down the foredeck and stood, one hand on the rail, listening to the music and watching the couples dancing reels on the main deck below. The three musicians leaned against the water casks, improvising their arrangements as they played. Young men and women stood around the edge, clapping their hands to the rhythm, and on the centre deck, ten couples bobbed up and down to the music. The men seemed young and strong and confident, and the women, dressed in their long gowns, were radiantly happy.

One tall woman in her early twenties was wearing a bright red dress. She had long dark hair that hung loosely to her shoulders. Her skin was pale and she had beautiful dark eyes, strong white teeth and a broad inviting smile. She seemed to be the attraction of the crowd, for at the end of each dance the others chatted to her excitedly.

Canso could not take his eyes off her. She seemed to be so lively, so beautiful, and yet so distant. For a long time he watched her every movement until she happened to look up on the foredeck and saw him looking at her. She smiled briefly and then went back to the dance. Except for an occasional quick glance at the foredeck she seemed determined to avoid the stares of the big sailor.

Gradually the weather had clouded over; the winter wind picked up speed, howling through the rigging and hurling spray onto the deck. The ship began to pitch in the waves of the Irish Sea. The music stopped and the dancers scurried for cover. While running for shelter, the young woman Canso had been watching looked up at him and gave him a full, dazzling smile. Then she disappeared into the steerage compartment below deck.

This seemed to bring Canso out of his thoughts. He turned to find Meg standing beside him. With an impish grin, Meg declared, "She likes you."

"What?" Canso said, startled to think that someone could so clearly read what was on his mind.

"She likes you. That's all said."

"I was just watching the dancers and ...." But Meg laughed at the sailor's awkward attempt to cover his feelings.

Suddenly the mate was shouting. "Stand by to cast off the towrope." He gave a signal to the steam tug. The rope went slack; four sailors unlooped it from the capstan and threw it over the bow and into the sea. The mate signalled that there was no need for the tug to come alongside and within moments the small vessel was steaming back to port, leaving the square-rigger alone.

"All hands set sail!" the mate ordered and the crew were into the shrouds scrambling as fast as they could for the royal yards. As each sail was unfolded, it swelled with the northwest wind and gradually the big square-rigger began to pitch through the waves on its southwest course.

CHAPTER 13

FOR the first two days of the voyage the *Scotian* rode before a stiff northwest wind. As she rounded the southern coast of Ireland and got into the open Atlantic, the wind shifted to the northeast and the ship plunged through heavy seas. The captain reefed the topsails and ran before the wind.

The passengers got a thorough rolling, but they soon settled into a pleasant routine and spirits were high. The captain appointed four of the middle-aged men to act as the passengers' committee, and in a friendly way they began enforcing the ship's rules and organizing the rotation of chores.

The day's activities began at seven in the morning when everyone was roused out of bed. The passengers rolled up their bedding and ten of the men swept out the steerage compartment, while the others took a turn about the deck for fresh air. At night everyone was to be in bed by nine and all the lanterns except one at the main hatchway were extinguished. Through the night the male passengers took three-hour shifts to check on irregularities and change the ventilation by opening and closing the hatches.

The passengers were expected to make most of their own meals. At breakfast Mr. Pepper and Meg measured out two quarts of water per adult, which was the day's ration, and a portion of oatmeal or potatoes depending on what they wanted. They would have to gather at the fireplaces on the foredeck to cook their meal. For dinner, Mr. Pepper prepared a beef or pork stew with potatoes and lots of dried bread. At supper the passengers again had to make their own meal of potatoes and griddlecakes.

Many of the people tried to spend as much time as possible on deck during the day. They would bundle up warmly against the cold December winds and exercise by walking on the deck or watching the sailors at their chores. The bosun or mate often took time out to explain the running of the ship to those that were curious but more frequently the people just lounged and chatted.

A good number of the passengers stayed below deck. It was much warmer, but the crowding and the dim light made it uncomfortable. Throughout the day young children played in the alleyways while the adults huddled around the candle lanterns or near the hatchways, reading books, playing the popular American card game of euchre, or talking with new acquaintances about the hopes and plans they had for their life in the New World.

After the supper meal, the impromptu band was assembled between decks and the dances were begun in the narrow passageways. For the young people this was a special time when they could court someone they fancied, but everyone — children, married couples, and old people alike — loved the party atmosphere.

Life was not so easy for the sailors during those days. The winds were irregular and there seemed to be a constant round of orders to shorten or take in sail. The conditions in the rigging were terrible. Strong winds howled constantly, and the ice-covered spars and ropes made the sailors' hands painfully cold. Every man had to be doubly cautious or he could find himself thrown from the ship.

Worst of all was the cursed, hateful pumping. At least twelve hours a day the sailors had to be at the pumps. No matter how rough the seas, or cold the winds, they had to stand at midships eternally working the handles up and down until it drained every ounce of their energy.

It was their second day out when Canso met Peggy Laing, the woman he had so admired the day they had left Liverpool. The mate's watch had been up in the rigging shortening sail, and when they came down, the Nova Scotian sailor found her standing at the rail near the shrouds. They started talking in the most natural way. John, José and Tommy were back at the pump, and they started work without their shipmate, but Mr. McKenzie noticed the sailor's absence.

"Back to work, Canso," he ordered gruffly. "And I'll thank you not to talk to the seamen please, madam."

In spite of the bad working conditions, all of the crew seemed to be more content in those first few days out of Liverpool, but the changes in Canso were remarkable. His brooding and hesitant manner was gone. Now he talked endlessly about the poor conditions of the ship and the way she sailed.

The only person aboard who seemed unaffected by the passengers was Captain Barnard. He paced the poop deck as before, watching the ocean and sky, carefully studying the running of his ship. He seemed to be oblivious to the feelings of those around him and the hardships and suffering of his crew. Rarely would he talk to anyone other than to give an order to a sailor on his watch, or to let the helmsman know that he had strayed off course.

The captain seemed intent on making the fastest crossing of the Atlantic possible. In spite of the age and condition of his ship, he would leave the canvas on her until it looked like a strong gust could pull the masts right out of the deck. The crew often complained about his tough manner but never did they balk at carrying out his orders.

On the fourth day out of port the barometer fell and the ship was into a fierce storm blowing from the northeast. It was biting cold and that night it began to snow heavily. A thirty-miles-an-hour wind, with fifty-miles-an-hour gusts, created mountainous waves off the starboard beam and the ship took a terrible rolling.

Still the captain would not stow all the sails or take them off course. He battened down the hatches, trapping the passengers below, and sailed before the wind with reefed foresail and close-reefed foretopsail. Often heavy seas broke over the deck and the water sloshed from side to side until the ship plunged into a trough, causing the water to rush through the scuppers and over the side.

The ship was taking on water heavily and with each watch the sailors had to stand at midships working the pumps, the rolling deck awash with water. They wore what warm clothing they had against the cold wind and pulled their oilskins over top, but still they got drenched. By the end of the watch the sailors were numb with cold.

Shelter in the forecastle offered little relief. The cramped room was without heat and all the sailors could do was strip off their wet clothing and huddle under the blankets, shivering violently until they fell into an exhausted sleep.

The passengers had a terrible time. Whenever Meg and Mr. Pepper went below to distribute food and water, the place seemed like a living hell. No fires could be lit on the deck and the emigrants had to survive on dry stale bread, hardtack and a little cheese. Scores of people were seasick. Already the air was foul from filthy bilge water, and the battened hatches made it impossible to get any fresh air into the compartment. To make matters worse, water leaked through the main deck onto the upper berths immediately below, soaking the beds thoroughly. By the second day of the storm the steerage was too dirty to sweep clean.

Those passengers who felt well enough kept distracted by sitting around lanterns placed on the long table that ran the centre of the ship, playing cards or reading, but there were many who felt so nauseous they did not even get out of bed. Morale was very low. People were bumped and bruised from being hurled from side to side with the lurching of the ship and more than one of the passengers were tossed from their berths when the ship was suddenly jarred.

It was hard for people who had no knowledge about ships or the sea not to be afraid at the moaning of the ship's timbers and the quivering of the masts as the *Scotian* plunged through the heavy waves. Some people cried, others prayed and many nasty arguments broke out as tempers were strained to the breaking point.

But after two days of the storm the barometer began to rise, the winds fell and the snow and sleet stopped. It was cold but at least the sailors could dress warmly and stay dry. On the morning of the sixth day out of Liverpool the mate ordered his watch to take off the hatches.

John and Canso struggled with the main hatch. After much effort it came up and they pushed it aside. The stench was overpowering to them and they sprang back in disbelief that anyone could live in such vile-smelling air. Impulsively Canso swung down the ladder and John followed. The two sailors could hardly believe the chaos. Baggage, pots and pans, tinware, dishes and every imaginable thing were strewn all about the alleyways. The people who just a few days before had seemed strong and optimistic about their future were now pale and unsteady, groping around in the dim light like helpless children.

The two sailors moved down the passageway urging the emigrants to get out of their berths and go above deck. A couple of older people were so unsteady they needed help and Canso easily lifted them down onto the deck, but some people, like the Irishwoman who had lied about her son's age, felt so weak they had to stay in bed. Most of the people, however, were roused and went above deck.

The passengers went back to their routine. Meg and Mr. Pepper doled out oatmeal and potatoes for breakfast and the fires were lit on the foredeck. The people stayed on deck as long as they could in an attempt to avoid the stinking steerage, but in time the cold December wind drove most of them back below again.

With the passengers on deck in the morning the pumping was delayed. The men of the mate's watch were seated on the main deck away from the emigrants milling around the fires, sewing up a new main royal sail to replace one that had been split in the storm. In spite of the cold it was a pleasant break to be away from the tedious job of manning the pumps.

While they worked, John looked up to see Peggy Laing standing between him and Canso. The boy grinned at her and she returned the greeting with a warm smile that lit up her whole face.

"Is it a good passage?" the boy asked shyly.

She shook her head and frowned. "It's terrible, terrible. I've never experienced conditions the like of it before." She spoke with a strong north country accent which gave a soft lilt to her voice. "What with the smashing of things and people crying I don't know if we can put up with another storm like that."

"There'll be worse to come," said Canso. "I've made the winter crossing of the Atlantic before and she's just one long string of storms."

Peggy frowned. "I don't look forward to it. Once the hatches are closed it truly becomes a nightmare."

"The cap'n doesn't make it any easier," added Canso. "He's not a man to ride out a storm. He sets her to the wind with as much canvas as she will stand and that gives the ship a terrible pounding."

"Is that why it is so rough?" Peggy asked

"Aye, that's one of the reasons," Canso replied.

"Is there anything we can do to help?" asked John.

"There's so many things that are wrong. Truth is that a ship like this should not be carrying passengers," Canso said decisively.

"That's true," said the boy. "Some of the crew wanted to report it to the authorities before we left Liverpool, but, well, we didn't do it." John glanced sharply at Canso wondering if the Nova Scotian seaman felt any guilt.

"It should have been done. There's no doubt of that." Peggy paused for a moment watching Canso sew neat stitches into the sail. "There is one thing," she went on, "the people sleeping right under the main deck got soaked in the storm with leaking water. There's no other place for them to move. Maybe if they could get some canvas to spread over the berths they could at least stay dry."

Canso looked up. "That should be possible. We have all sorts of canvas aboard." He spotted the bosun up on the foredeck and sent John to get him. When they returned, Canso proposed that the canvas should be given to the people. Mr. Ryerson promised to ask the captain about it. Two hours later the bosun reported that the master rejected the request because it would be too expensive. Canso cursed under his breath knowing there was nothing that would change the decision. But John was glad to see the sailor angry. This was more like the Canso that they had first met.

The conditions of the passengers were of real concern to some of the crew. John, Meg, Canso and Mr. Pepper spent as much of their spare time as possible in the steerage compartment trying to help those that were unable to help themselves. They scrounged blankets for those too poor to afford them and they organized others to cook meals for those too sick to go to the fireplaces on the foredeck.

The cramped quarters and meagre rations were causing trouble. Some of the younger men became unruly and uncooperative. The passenger committee was unable to get them to do their share of the work, and more than once there were ugly scenes at the fireplaces or in steerage.

One evening, when the mate's watch was manning the pumps, a violent argument broke out between a young Yorkshireman who had been drinking heavily and the middle-aged father of five hungry young children. The young man pushed his way into line, putting his cake on the griddle. The argument quickly turned to shoving, and then punches were thrown.

Quick as he could Canso was up on the deck and pulled the two men apart with his great strength. "You'll keep to your turn or you'll deal with me," he shouted at the young man. "There's enough problems on this voyage without fighting with each other."

In those desperate days it seemed as if Canso was the only one aboard ship who could still command respect from everyone. Peggy Laing was constantly coming to him with problems of the passengers and John and Meg both noticed that the crew once again treated him as if he was their real leader.

Captain Barnard became more and more remote. Often he would receive delegations from the passengers requesting special concessions or altered conditions, but he was impervious to it all. The passengers came to see him as arrogant and aloof, for he was obsessed with his ship. The only thing that was important to him was to get the *Scotian* to Halifax.

The good weather lasted only two days and then a storm rising out of the southeast swept down on them. The captain refused to stow all the sails and tried to run before the wind, but the ship developed a frightening roll as she took the waves off the larboard beam. To the seamen the dirty weather meant more pumping. For sixteen hours a day, four hours on and four off, the sailors had to lash themselves to the pump handle to keep the hull dry. By the end of each four-hour watch they were wet, cold and completely worn-out.

That night, with the gale howling through the rigging and wet snow and freezing rain driving out of the northeast, the call of "All hands to stow sails" was given. There was a half inch of thick ice covering everything as the crew began climbing the shrouds. Slowly they inched their way out on the yards, with the wind tugging at their oilskins and the rain lashing at their face and hands. The night was inky black. The ice-encrusted foot and hand ropes were slippery and freezing cold. At any moment it seemed as if someone might lose their grip and be thrown into the turbulent sea. The sailors loosened the mainsail. It cracked violently against the mast; they pulled on the buntlines, but the ice lent the sail an enormous weight. It was difficult but finally the seamen had the sail furled around the yard.

Once it was lashed into place, the crew were back into the shrouds, climbing to the lower topsail. John found that the conditions got worse the higher they climbed. The masts plunged back and forth violently with each wave; the wind tore at them in an effort to pull them from their perch. The boy's hands were chafed and sore, but he held on tightly until finally all the canvas was stowed. Like the others, he survived to return to the forecastle and thoroughly condemn the captain for leaving the sails on for so long.

All through the night Canso struggled with the ship, keeping her head pointed directly into the wind and wrestling to control her through every wave. It seemed to John that Canso alone was the one who was keeping the ship together. Beside him was the captain, lashed to the rail, watching his ship labour through the heavy seas without saying a word. And all night long the watches took turns, lashing themselves to the pump for four-hour shifts, desperately trying to keep the vessel dry.

With dawn, the violence of the storm continued but the snow and freezing rain stopped. In spite of the exhaustion of the crew the captain ordered the jibs and lower topsails set. Once they were secured, Canso brought the ship around, set her back on course, and the *Scotian* began plunging through the heavy seas again.

Ten hours after he had taken the helm, Canso was relieved by Georges, and the captain let the crew stay in the forecastle for one watch. The entire crew were so tired it was all they could do to pull off their wet clothes and fall asleep.

No sooner had they settled when Meg came into the forecastle looking for Canso. She and Mr. Pepper had gone down into the steerage compartment with the morning's rations and had found the place in chaos. Peggy Laing had come up to her and had begged her to find Canso. In spite of his exhaustion Canso began dressing without hesitation. John also got dressed, and the three of them went below.

The steerage was in terrible condition. The smell from the bilge water was so overpowering that both Meg and John gagged. People had been vomiting everywhere. The roof over the main deck had leaked badly and water sloshed back and forth on the floor with each plunge of the ship.

The passengers were distressed. Children and women were sobbing. Many people lay still in their bunks, staring through vague, hopeless eyes, while others slopped in the ankle-deep water poking among the debris, searching for their belongings.

Peggy met them at the bottom of the ladder. "I'm sorry to have called you, Canso, but the passengers surely believe that the end is near." The strain seemed to give a stronger lilt to her accent. "Last night 'twas like a nightmare. People thrown out of their bunks, their beds soaked, the ship creaking and groaning like she was about to break up. You've got to do something, Canso!"

The Nova Scotian sailor touched her dark hair lightly. "Things will be all right. It's a bad storm, but the ship rode it out well."

"But Canso, don't just say that." Her eyes flashed with anger. "You must help these people. We can talk and talk all we like but you must do something!"

The seaman sighed. "Aye. You're right, Peggy. It's time the captain and I spoke about many things."

Canso's voice and the set of his shoulders told John and Meg that this time he meant it.

CHAPTER 14

IT did not take long for Canso to get agreement from the crew that they should take their grievances to the captain. Without exception, every sailor felt hostility about the running of the ship and wanted to see major changes. At three that afternoon, when the captain's watch was manning the pumps, all the members of the crew met on the main deck and went aft to confront their master.

Heavy seas rolled in on the larboard beam and the wind whistling through the rigging made it difficult to talk. The sailors held onto the mizzenmast and the rail while Canso had it out with the captain. John and Meg strained to hear what was said.

"The crew have been talking things over, Cap'n," the Nova Scotian sailor began. "We're here to settle our grievances with you."

Captain Barnard looked guardedly from man to man. "Are you plotting mutiny, Canso?"

"We intend no mutiny Cap'n, but we do intend that you hear us out." Canso's attitude allowed the captain no alternative. "We feel that you're driving the *Scotian* too hard. She won't take this treatment. We're running those cursed pumps eighteen hours a day now and we're at the point where we can't take it any more. If she gets any worse, then we'll be floundering. We've got a load of passengers, and we shouldn't be taking these chances. We should head back to Galway or Cork or Liverpool while we can still make it."

"No! Never! We're Halifax bound and we'll make it even if you have to pump every minute of every hour until we're there."

"But what if she flounders, Cap'n?" Canso asked.

"She'll not flounder. I know my ship." The master's eyes were bloodshot. Tired lines set his mouth and eyes into a deep frown. "You sailors don't seem to understand. Once I get this ship to Halifax she'll be mine. If we go back I'll have to refund the passengers and that will ruin me."

"It's a terrible chance you are taking," said Canso

"That's my worry. You're paid to work, nothing else," the Captain stated flatly.

The seaman looked back at the others. They still looked determined to win some concessions. Canso looked back to their master. "The destination of the ship may be up to you. Certainly none of the passengers want to turn back. But what about the pumping? And the passengers who have berths right below the main deck? They are getting a soaking. The least we could do is give them pieces of canvas so they could stay dry."

"I have no canvas to spare. Those people knew this passage would not be easy. They'll have to put up with it. As for the pumping, there's many an able-bodied man among the emigrants. I'll ask the passengers' committee if we can have some volunteers. Would that be all right?"

A number of the men nodded. To be relieved of the exhausting job of pumping would be welcome, but they stood their ground without showing any expression.

"All right then, we're agreed." The captain hesitated as if uncertain of himself "You must understand. We must get this ship through to Halifax . . . ." His voice trailed off, but then he tried again. "You mustn't think badly of me. I am only doing what I must do." But the blank expressionless looks on the faces of the crew must have made him recognize that they would no longer listen to his explanations.

As the men went back to their chores they were grumbling that they had not been able to gain any more concessions, but John could not help but feel that they had made big gains. There was a sense of urgency about the captain that he had never shown before. For the first time he was concerned what the crew thought of him and there was even the indication that he was willing to listen to their complaints.

The captain kept to his word and talked to the passengers' committee about organizing the young men into teams of pumpers. They seemed glad to do it. Many of the men were fed up with spending long hours trapped in the hold and welcomed the chance to do a job that required use of their muscles.

At the same time, it gave the crew a chance to rest up, and they were able to devote more time to tasks that they had neglected, such as sewing patches on ripped sails and checking to see that everything was in order aloft.

For the next five days there was no improvement in the weather, making it impossible for the passengers. Throughout this period the hatches were battened down, trapping them below deck. Meg and Mr. Pepper went down at meal time to distribute the rations but no one was allowed to go above deck to prepare meals. Christmas came and went with no ceremony to mark it from any other day. The complaints mounted about the monotonous diet of bread, hardtack and cheese, and the squalor suffered by the three hundred and sixty people trapped in one compartment became intolerable.

John, Meg, Canso and occasionally a few other sailors would go below when they were off watch to help the passengers in any way that they could. More than once Canso could be found with Peggy Laing, but he also talked to a variety of passengers, and he soon became known by everyone in steerage. To them he was a big, happy, optimistic man undaunted by the troubles around him. As soon as Canso came into the hold he would be surrounded by emigrants asking about the ship, the weather and their progress to Halifax. The seaman took a special interest in those who were sick, stopping by their berths to ask how they were, and frequently he would sit with the children telling them stories about the sea.

John and Meg were both struck by the change that had come over the sailor. Once, when the three of them were alone in the mess, John asked him about it.

"It's strange," the big man replied. "It's as if I have some sense of purpose now. I have something to look forward to."

"But I don't understand," said Meg. "Sometimes you don't tell the truth to the passengers. You say things are fine aboard ship."

"They look up to me, don't you see that, Meg? I'm the one who tells them about the running of the ship and what's happening above deck. I just don't have the heart to tell them the truth. What if I told them the ship's taking on too much water, or the cap'n's half mad? They'd get panicky and expect at any moment the ship would break up. It's better this way."

The next day things took a turn for the worse for the people in steerage. There was a very bad infestation of lice that spread rapidly in the bedclothes. It got into people's hair and clothes, and soon, no matter how clean the people had tried to keep themselves, they were badly bitten.

Some felt that if they could only wash their bedding and clothes they could get rid of the vermin, and the passengers' committee was sent to see the captain to ask for a greater ration of water. They had disappointing news when they returned. Water was running short and there would be no washing of any kind allowed. Some of the people resorted to washing their hair in vinegar to get rid of the lice, but it did little good.

The next day an epidemic of diarrhea spread among the passengers. Many of them were very sick and weak but there was little that they could do, other than lie moaning in their berths. The ship's doctor was called, but he had no adequate medicine aboard and knew so little about disease that he was next to useless. Rumour circulated that he had never been to medical school and was in fact a doctor's assistant whom the passenger broker had put on board to fulfill the regulations.

It was Canso who thought that the diarrhea was probably caused by bad water, and he told everyone that it should not be drunk until it was boiled. But since they could not get out on deck, there was no way to boil it. Canso talked to Mr. Pepper and arranged that a small group of women could come into the galley to boil water for everyone.

The sickness took a serious toll. Some of the people seemed barely touched by it, but others, like the Irish woman who was sick before, developed a very high fever. Peggy Laing organized the single people to do what they could for the sick, but other than bringing them food and giving comfort there was little that could be done.

That afternoon the barometer began to drop alarmingly and by night an intense storm swept down on them. The passengers were poorly equipped to be out on deck in wet conditions so the sailors, dressed in their oilskins and southwesters, had to resume the task of pumping. A bitter cold wind howling out of the northeast drove a mixture of snow, sleet and freezing rain before it. The waves swelled and the wind tore off their tops, sending them flying in driving sheets.

Meg was called out of the galley by the captain and was sent to fetch Canso to take over the wheel. Ice and snow were already caked on the deck as she struggled forward. She waited in the forecastle as he struggled on with his oilskins.

"It's a dirty night out there, Canso," she remarked.

The Nova Scotian sailor seemed angry. “The cap’n’s a fool. He’s still trying to run before the wind with sails set. With every wave, she jars so that it feels like she’ll fall apart. I’ll tell you I’ll not take the helm unless he rides out the storm.”

On deck the two leaned into the bitter wind and driving snow and rain. They went hand over hand along the rail so they would not lose footing on the slippery deck. With an effort they climbed up to the poop deck and back to the helm.

Scobie, who was manning the wheel, was glad to see them, but Canso went directly to the captain. In the dim light Meg could see the master’s red-ringed eyes and tired face.

Canso had to shout in order to be heard. “I’ll not take over the wheel unless we strip the sails. It’s just too dangerous, Cap’n. The ice is too heavy and the wind is too strong. The masts will come down. We could lose the ship.” He sounded as if he had finally made up his mind and was determined to stick by it.

“You’re to follow my orders, Canso. If you don’t, I’ll put you in irons.”

“Damn your irons!” he shouted. “I’ll not have a hand in the sinking of this ship!”

The captain seized the rail with both hands and looked far out into the darkness of the sea. When he turned back, the tension in his face made his eyes and mouth twitch involuntarily. “You don’t understand, Canso. You just don’t understand. I’ve got to get this ship through to Halifax. We’ve been out of Liverpool for over two weeks now and we’ve been sailing through storm after storm, but still we're just a little over halfway. The ship is taking on so much water we can't keep it dry. We've got to take advantage of every wind we can get."

Canso seemed stunned, as the full implication of the captain's words began to sink in. "You mean … " he began, but his voice trailed off.

However, the captain's words were understandable even to Meg, who had overheard them. As the hull began filling with water, the windjammer had slowed because of the added weight. They were now involved in a race with their own ship to get across the Atlantic. If the water leaked in any faster there was no saving her. The *Scotian* would sink deeper and deeper into the waves until there was nothing that they could do other than abandon ship. With three hundred and sixty passengers aboard, the thought of taking to open boats on the North Atlantic in mid-winter was too frightening to contemplate.

"Can't we run for Iceland?" shouted Canso, desperately searching for an answer.

"Too far. And the prevailing winds in the North Atlantic are from the northeast in the winter. It's faster to head due west." The captain paused for a moment. "Do you understand now, Canso? We've got to leave every sail on her that she can possibly take, or we'll be at the bottom of the sea."

"We should have re-caulked her in Kingston like I wanted."

Captain Barnard could not look Canso in the eye. "I know. You were right … but I had to pay for my ship and …." His voice was lost to the wind.

Slowly Canso took the captain's arm. The master seemed older now and more tired, as if the act of letting someone share his terrible secret was a relief to him. But what could they do? Now was not the time to assign blame. The mistakes had been made; the errors committed. Their survival depended on everyone.

"Don't worry, Cap'n," said Canso reassuringly. "We'll get to Halifax. We'll win the race if we all work together."

The captain's weary smile was a signal that he accepted the seaman's offer of help.

Canso relieved Scobie at the helm, tying himself to the binnacle and holding the spoked wheel in his two massive arms. In spite of the freezing rain and driving wind the other sailors kept up their pumping without stopping. It took all their energy, but they never seemed to be getting anywhere. Every four hours, with the bell ringing to mark the change of the watch, the dark forms of the sailors would be replaced by another group dressed exactly the same way.

Everything was covered in thick, glistening ice. Even the two big mainsails that were left up were encrusted, but the wind was so strong that they did not ever sag. The sailors, working the pumps, speculated how long it would take before one of the yards, unable to take the extra weight, would come crashing down on the deck.

Sometime around midnight an electrical storm began that added to the violence. With each flash of lightning the ghostly ship was bathed in an eerie light, revealing glistening spars and rigging encrusted with ice, black-suited sailors working the pumps and two forms huddled around the wheel.

The storm came closer and closer to the ship. Deafening cracks of thunder were followed immediately by almost blinding flashes and then, suddenly, lightning struck the mainmast. Another flash showed the top of the mast splintered and dangling high above the deck, threatening to hurtle down at any moment.

For the first time in weeks Captain Barnard took real leadership of his crew. He gathered the hands that were on duty at the pump back to the poop deck and explained his plan. "We have to get the broken part of the mast down. If it falls it'll crash through the deck and onto the passengers. When this electrical storm passes, we'll go up and cut it loose and ease it down onto the deck."

"How about the sails, Cap'n?" shouted José.

"They stay on."

"But Cap'n."

"They stay on," said Canso. "I'll explain later."

John was sent below to call the bosun and the mate. Others went to collect equipment from the storeroom. The sailors waited silently for fifteen minutes until the electrical storm passed off to the south of them. Then the wheel was turned over to the bosun. Canso took an axe, the mate brought a heavy rope and the captain led the way into the mainmast shrouds.

John was as frightened as he had ever been before, but he followed without hesitation. The shrouds and ratlines were covered in half an inch of ice, making it very slippery and dangerous. The further they climbed, the more the wind and driving sleet pulled at their bodies and cut into their hands and faces.

Quickly the mate put a hitch around the broken section with the rope that he had brought, and lashed it securely to the icy mainmast. Then Canso worked his way through the rigging until he was at the spot where the mast was broken. With one hand he held on and with the other he lashed himself in place. Taking the axe he severed the mast with four powerful blows. As it came loose, it slipped and seemed for a moment as if it would crash down onto the deck. But then the mate's rope held.

The task of lowering the mast to the deck was a nightmare. They loosened the rope, and with every sailor holding on, they slowly lowered the heavy timber until it became entangled in the rigging. Then it would be lashed into place and one of the sailors would have to lower himself down until he could cut it free with his knife. Then they would lower it until again it became entangled. After what seemed like hours of work they had the mast safely onto the deck. Everyone was so exhausted that the captain sent them all below and called the other watch to man the pumps.

At dawn the ship was wakened to the cry of "All hands set sail! All hands set sail!" It was a beautiful day. In spite of the cold, the sun was up in a clear blue sky, and the seas had fallen to an easy roll. Within half an hour the sailors had set every sail on the *Scotian* except the main royal sail, which had come down in the storm. The ship gained speed and plunged through the seas making a foam at her clipper bow.

The order was given to open the hatches and let the passengers come on deck. The sailors quickly worked the hatches free and after giving the foul air a moment to clear, Canso, John and Meg went below.

The plight of the passengers was pathetic. Belongings of every kind were scattered about. Water sloshed two inches deep on the floor. The passengers, pale and weak from being locked below for so long, stumbled along the alleyways trying to adjust their eyes to the harsh sunlight that poured in from the hatchway.

"Everyone up on deck! The weather's fine!" Canso shouted. Gradually the excitement of the emigrants rose as they realized that they would get out of their prison after five full days of confinement.

But then Peggy Laing came slowly down the passageway. "Canso, be still will ye?" she said quietly. "It's the Irishwoman. She's dead."

CHAPTER 15

A board lay so that one end was on the larboard rail and the other on the main deck. On top of it the dead Irishwoman's body was sewn into a white canvas sack that Canso had made for her. Around the form stood the woman's husband and her seventeen-year-old son; beyond them were the passengers and crew of the *Scotian*, gathered to give their last respects to the dead.

Captain Barnard stood solemnly at the body's head, reading the service out of the Common Prayer Book. He was dressed in his best dark suit with his hat under his arm. The tired, haggard look of his eyes and face reflected the strain of the voyage.

Only snatches of the prayer were heard: "Commit her body to the deep … when the sea shall give up her dead …." The rest was lost in the sound of the wind and rush of the sea along the ship's hull.

In spite of the simplicity of the service, and the mixed beliefs of those present, everyone felt a deep sadness that this woman, who had yearned so much for a better life for herself and her family, had not lived to see her dreams realized.

When he had finished, the captain closed the prayer book and the relatives, passengers and crew stood silently for a moment. Then, at the captain's nod, José and

Santana lifted the board into the air, and the weighted canvas sack and its contents slid silently overboard, sinking quietly into the depths of the sea.

The captain briefly whispered condolences and returned to the poop deck. Slowly the passengers and crew went back to their work and chores that they had left behind, leaving the old man and his son to stare vacantly at the sea as if they were still trying to understand what had happened to them.

For the next few days the wind came steadily out of the southeast. It was overcast and occasionally there was drizzling rain, but the crew was thankful that it was warmer than it had been since they had left Liverpool. All canvas was set, and they sailed before a brisk wind, but still the *Scotian* did not have much speed. In spite of constant pumping they could not get the ship dry. The added weight of the water made her lumber through the waves as if she was carrying the heaviest cargo possible.

Every morning the cook and Meg distributed the meagre rations. At breakfast and supper, people scrambled around the fires trying to produce something edible to fill their hungry stomachs. Arguments became more and more frequent until the passengers' committee had to put someone on the foredeck at all times to settle disputes. The only real meal they had was the dumpling stew Mr. Pepper made at noon and even that was severely rationed.

The first sign of panic from the passengers began when the rats started swarming out of the hold. It began slowly at first. One of the women saw a pair scurrying for cover and shouted in panic. Over the next few days, more and more rats were sighted until one evening they seemed to be coming out by the hundreds.

At first some of the young men found sport in hunting them, but the longer it went on the greater were the numbers. People were frightened of being bitten and there was a growing fear they would spread disease.

When the rat infestation became out of control, Peggy Laing sought out Canso. "I don't understand it," she said. "Why are they coming out all at the same time?" The tone of her voice showed her own fear.

Canso glanced uneasily at John who was beside him. "I don't know, Peggy. Let's go down and see."

In their short visit the two seamen spotted five rats. Canso tried to treat it casually as if this was a normal occurrence aboard ship, but he offered the passengers no explanation.

Once they were back out on deck alone the big seaman swore under his breath. "Do you see what's happening, boy? Because we can't keep the ship pumped dry, the bilge water is filling up the hold. The rats, who live down there, are getting flooded out. To escape they're coming up into the steerage compartment."

"What can we do about it?"

"Not much. But the real problem is that some of the passengers might figure out what's happening. Then, God knows, a panic might start."

Canso spoke to the captain and mate. They both were very concerned and left the discussion shaking their heads gravely. Canso and the other members of the mate's watch were sent below with lumber, hammers and nails to try to block up any possible opening where the rats could escape, but it seemed to make little difference. Soon the rodents were swarming everywhere on the ship. Occasionally they would be seen on the main deck and on one occasion John found a rat scrambling up the mainmast as if intent on finding safety.

The day after the plague of rats began the passengers noticed that there was water on the floor of the between-decks. At first they could not understand it. During rain storms, water leaked through the main deck and sloshed around on the floor of the steerage compartment until it drained into the hold, but it had not been raining for days.

Slowly it dawned on some of the passengers that the water was coming from the bilge. The hold was almost full now and as the ship rolled from side to side in the waves, some water leaked up through the floorboards. Some of the emigrants figured out that this meant that in spite of the around-the-clock pumping the ship was filling up with water.

John heard groups of emigrants on deck talking about it.

"She's going down, I tell you!" one of the young men was telling a member of the passengers' committee. "They can't pump her dry. That means that the ship will just fill up more and more and then she'll just sink."

"No! I don't believe it. The cap'n wouldn't do that to us."

"I tell you it's true. Look for yourself."

Within two hours the rumour had spread to all the ship's passengers and they were panicking. A large group of them, who had been on the foredeck, suddenly resolved to see the captain. They stormed across the main deck, seventy-five strong, up to the poop deck, and began shouting at the master.

Peggy had been talking to John when this happened and she told him to get Canso, and then quickly followed the group.

John found the capable sailor in one of the storage rooms. "Hurry up, Canso!" he shouted. "It's the passengers. They found out!"

The seamen rushed aft as quickly as they could, to find the captain surrounded by an angry, shouting mob.

"We're sinking, Cap'n! Isn't that right?" one aggressive man was shouting.

"We're taking on more water than we can pump out."

"Will we have to abandon ship?"

"You're a fraud, Cap'n. You got us on an unsafe ship."

"You'll be the first to die! Mark my word!"

Captain Barnard bravely confronted the panicking mob. "No! No! We're not going to sink. Control yourselves. Let me speak!"

But the mob was too angry. "Are we going under, Captain?" someone shouted. "Should we abandon ship?" The panic was rising.

"Stop it! Stop it right now!" Canso shouted at the top of his voice. He had climbed a little way up the mizzen shroud so everyone could see him. "Listen to what the captain has to say. If you panic, then we all will surely die." The crowd grew silent. "Everyone get back to the main deck so the captain can stand at the poop rail and explain things to you."

"We want to know exactly what's happening!" someone yelled. There were loud shouts of agreement.

"You'll get your answers but first we have to have some order or everything will be lost. Now let's get down to the main deck, please."

Canso's leadership had brought some calm. Slowly the people filed down to the main deck, others were called from below and soon the entire population of the *Scotian* was assembled.

Captain Barnard began nervously, but the longer he spoke the more confidence he showed. "You have learned the terrible secret. Now everyone knows that the *Scotian* is slowly floundering. But this does not mean that we're about to abandon ship. That would be madness. A ship can sail with a hold half full of water for days and days without fear of sinking. It may get uncomfortable, the water may come up into the compartment, but we'll keep pumping day and night and I swear to you that we'll be able to make it to Halifax."

There was angry shouting when the captain had finished. "You should have told us, Captain!" "Why were you allowed to carry passengers?" "Why don't you come below and live with bilge water and rats?"

"Quiet!" the captain shouted above the uproar. "You will have to trust us. My crew and I will be doing everything possible to get you safely to Halifax, but you must help. We must all work together. We need volunteers to man the pumps. We need people to help maintain order in the passengers' compartment, and above all we need you to remain calm. If you cannot do that, then we are all lost."

A new confidence went through the company. The captain's firm decisiveness made the passengers feel they were in good hands, and gradually they disappeared below deck satisfied that everything possible had been done. That afternoon the captain instituted a new schedule for pumping. All able-bodied men were conscripted into the chore and two-hour shifts around the clock were arranged. The men were instructed that they were to pump as fast as they possibly could. For a time it seemed as if the water level was dropping a little, but by morning there was a good three inches of water sloshing about on the floor of the between-decks.

Conditions were terrible for the passengers. Their belongings were drenched. Rats competed with them for dry spaces on the bunk beds and tables, and the plague of lice returned. Those on the lower berths could not sleep without being splashed with dirty bilge water every time the ship pitched into a wave. The only thing to quench their thirst was putrid water laced with vinegar to make it drinkable. Constant hunger made them irritable. The rations served out every morning grew smaller and smaller and the cook's stew got so thin that it was soup. The only thing left in any quantity was flour and oatmeal, so the emigrants fashioned it into a sort of griddlecake, which they cooked over the fires and ate, burned on the outside and raw on the inside.

At dawn of one morning six weeks into the voyage, the captain called Meg to help him take navigation readings. When they pulled in the log which measured the speed of the boat, they found that the *Scotian* had slowed to three knots an hour despite a stiff northern breeze. But after the captain had done his calculations with the sextant, he seemed more confident.

"We should make it, Meg," he said with a smile. "We're only seventy-five miles off the Nova Scotia coast."

"That should make you very happy," Meg said, a little sharply.

"Now Meg, don't you be unkind. I owe a lot to you. Remember the argument we had in the streets of Liverpool?"

"When I called you a greedy old fool?" Meg said, a smile at her lips.

"Aye, well there was truth in it. But you said other things which made me think deeply, and quite right you were. No man can run a ship alone. Not if he wants to get home safe and sound."

"Home!" Meg said softly, looking toward the west. "I can't believe it!"

As the morning wore on there were a number of indications that they were close to some shore. Seabirds were flying close to the water and some passengers spotted a big fish off the starboard bow.

That afternoon the weather took a turn for the worse. By four o'clock it had begun to snow and visibility was reduced to a quarter of a mile. Captain Barnard paced the deck nervously. Soon it would be dark and because of the weather he could not get an accurate navigational reading. Finally he gave the order to stow all sails. They would drift all night until he could get another sighting on the sun the next morning and locate their position.

It was pitch dark at six o'clock the next morning when John was called out of his bunk by the mate to take his turn as lookout. The boy dressed in his oilskins and southwester and went out on deck. Three inches of snow covered the deck and a strong breeze drove out of the northeast. The sea was running high, but José at the wheel kept the *Scotian* pointed into the waves and she rode easily up and down with each swell. On the main deck four of the passengers, warmly dressed against the elements, rapidly worked the pumps.

John climbed up to the bow and looked into the face of the storm. The swirling snow made it difficult to see more than a few feet over the prow, but there was a faint hint of dawn that greyed the sky. Then he walked aft, careful to hold onto the rail for fear that he would lose his footing on the slippery, snow-covered deck. The mate and José stood at the wheel talking. John listened for a few moments and then began making his way forward again.

It was as he was about to go down the ladder to the main deck that he first sensed that something was wrong. He stopped, straining to listen. He thought he heard the sound of thunder, but that did not seem possible. He had just about dismissed the idea when he heard it again. This time he was certain.

He sprang into the starboard mizzen shrouds and climbed twenty-five feet into the rigging. The dawn had lightened the sky even more now but still the heavy snow made it difficult to see more than the length of the ship. Then he heard the sound again and realized what it was.

"Stop the pumps!" John shouted anxiously down to the mate.

"What for?"

"Just get them to stop."

A moment later there was silence. The boy strained to hear. Yes, he was sure of it now. It was the crash of waves breaking against the shore due west of the ship. A moment later it was light enough to see the white outline of a snow-covered shore no more than two hundred yards away.

"Land ho!" he shouted excitedly. "Land ho!"

CHAPTER 16

ALL hands on deck! All hands on deck!" the mate shouted at the top of his voice. Then he raced forward to make sure the sailors heard him in the forecastle.

The seamen struggled onto the deck on the double. The captain was still buttoning up his blue jacket as he hurried out of his quarters. "Great God!" he shouted in horror as he saw their position.

The snow was still falling, but visibility was clear enough to make out the rocky, barren shore a hundred and fifty yards away. Immediately to the north was a long arm of land stretching seaward which blocked any escape. As far south as they could see was a broken rocky coastline edged in white foam from breakers that pounded in from the North Atlantic.

The crew stood midships anxiously waiting for a command from their master. The captain moved from side to side of the poop deck by the helm. It seemed to take an eternity, but at last he shouted decisively. "Rig all jibs! Set the main mizzen sail! Canso, take the helm!"

Santana, Hans and Scobie ran to the prow to set the jibs. Canso raced to take over the helm. The captain loosened the rope to the mizzen sail threading it through the block.The crew leaned into the rope and the sail opened with a crack. Canso put the wheel over to starboard. They would try to take the *Scotian* back to the deep water on a southeast tack.

The sailors waited. The wind filled the mizzen sail and the ship started to go over on her starboard beam. It seemed as if the wind might take them, but just as Canso fixed the tack, a large wave caught them on the larboard bow and pushed the ship toward the shore.

"Hard over, Canso! Hard over!" shouted the captain.

The sailor brought her more to the south, the wind filled the sail and again it seemed for a moment as if it might be enough to take them into the deep water. But a wave caught her midships, again pushing her toward shore, and John realized that the water in the ship's hold carried too much weight for the wind to move them.

"Set the forward mainsail!" the captain shouted desperately. The crew ran as fast as they could go. Within a minute they had loosened the big sail, unfurled it and tied it down. The canvas filled with wind but just as they thought they had enough sail to take them away from shore another wave pushed them further toward the rocky beach.

"Set the forward topsails!" shouted the captain. The crew worked feverishly, but even when these were rigged, it seemed as if they were not winning the battle. With each wave pounding in against them, the ship slipped closer and closer toward shore.

The captain rushed back to the helm. "What's happening, Canso?"

"She's not pulling out to sea, Cap'n. The weight in the hold is too much for the sails."

They were less than a hundred yards from shore now, and in spite of the canvas, each wave pushed them closer and closer. At any moment they could hit an underwater ridge that might spill the ship over on its side; within moments she might be pounded to pieces. Would they have time to rig more canvas? Was there enough wind to get them back out to sea? What were the chances? Suddenly the captain made his decision.

"Anchors aweigh!" he shouted. "Anchors aweigh! Cut away the sails!"

The sailors knew exactly what to do. In an instant they leapt into the rigging and slashed the ropes holding the sails with their knives so that they flapped harmlessly in the wind. At the same time others raced for the bow, and within moments the two big anchors which had been lashed to the deck fell into the sea. The chains rattled as they played out and then as the anchors settled, the captain ordered that they both be tied off around the capstan.

Canso had brought the bow into the waves again and the ship drifted, her stern toward the shore. Everyone waited, watching the anchor chains grow taut, wondering if they could hold the weight of the ship and the pounding of the waves. Finally she came to the end of the length of chain and seemed to be holding.

"All hands aft!" the captain ordered.

Within moments the seamen were gathered around the helm. All the crew were there, including Meg and Mr. Pepper. Tension tightened their faces. Without saying a word, every member knew the seriousness of their situation. Less than a hundred yards away was a rocky beach, barren and inhospitable, which could crush their wooden ship to pieces within minutes.

The snow had stopped but there was no sign that the wind howling through the riggings would moderate. The waves driving in from the open North Atlantic were battering the hull of the water-sodden ship. No one knew how long the anchors would hold but chances were that they could not take that enormous pressure for long.

Some of the crew were close to panic but Captain Barnard's decisive leadership gave them hope. "We're going to get the passengers ashore," he shouted above the wind. "Mr. Mckenzie, take Georges and Santana forward and begin playing out the anchor chains until I give you a hand signal to stop. That will make the run into shore closer. Canso, you take the rest of the crew and start loosening the two lifeboats off their blocks." The sailors immediately began to execute these orders.

The four passengers who had been manning the pumps were on the main deck during all of this action. Their fear had immobilized them as they watched the crew battle to take the ship back out to the open sea. When the anchors were dropped, they finally understood the danger to them. The four of them pried off the hatchway and went below shouting to the passengers that they were about to be shipwrecked on a rocky shore.

Panic ripped through the passengers' quarters. There was a mad rush to the hatchways. People were squeezed and pushed as they tried to scramble up the ladder. One child was knocked down into the cold bilge water by the mob and might have been crushed had not Peggy Laing rescued him.

When they got on deck they rushed as one body to the rails and peered in disbelief at the shore. Wild shrieks and deafening cries pierced the air as the whole group of people came to believe that their end was near. Some were in their night clothes, many were in bare feet without their coats on, and all were terrified that at any moment the ship was about to be crushed to pieces on the shore.

Suddenly a young man shrieked, "To the boats!" and, as if by a single will, the crowd surged up to the poop deck where the lifeboats were kept. Canso, John and the other sailors were attempting to get the boats off their blocks and swing them over the side so they could be lowered into the sea once they were loaded. The surge of people pushed them aside. Those that could manage, scrambled into the boats and sat waiting as if by this act alone they thought they could be saved. The others thronged the deck, frantically looking for any means of escape.

All of the crew members tried to stop them, but without success. Canso climbed up the sides of one of the whalers and shouted as loudly as he could. "You'll have to get out of the boats! We won't even be able to get them over the side with you in them. Please! If you have any hope to save yourself, we'll have to get these boats free!"

But in spite of the respect many of the passengers had for Canso, they would not budge. Everyone aboard ship knew that there were not enough lifeboats for all the passengers and they believed that if they gave up their places they would go down with the ship. Canso was desperate. The crew could never physically throw all of those people out of the boats.

Suddenly there was a deafening explosion of a gun, and then another. The captain had climbed into the mizzen rigging and was pointing a revolver down at the people in one of the whalers. "Get out of the boat!" he shouted feverishly. "Get out now or you'll never get off this ship alive!" It looked as if he would pull the trigger at any moment.

The passengers sat for a moment uncertain what to do. Then one of the men put his leg over the side and dropped back to the deck. Another followed reluctantly and then each one of them went over the side until the whaler was emptied. The captain waved his gun threateningly in the direction of the other boat and they followed suit.

Captain Barnard called out to the panic-stricken passengers from his position in the rigging. "We must keep calm or we are lost. We have a good chance to save every life aboard ship, but those who try to save only themselves endanger everyone. Go back below and dress warmly. Bring blankets if you have them. Then wait on the main deck. But please calm yourselves."

As the passengers left the poop deck, the sailors tried to encourage them. "Don't lose heart." "We can still save ourselves." But even so, there was fear in their voices.

Meg noticed that as Peggy Laing passed Canso she squeezed his hand and smiled just for an instant.

The captain signalled to the mate at the bow of the ship and slowly they began letting out the anchor chains. The ship drifted closer and closer to shore. The sound of the waves pounding on the rocky beach was deafening. Meg, standing close to the rail, worried that they might get too close, but finally the captain signalled the mate by waving his hands and the anchor chains were tied off.

The *Scotian* felt very unstable. Her bow was pointed into the huge waves and her stern toward shore. She swayed back and forth, tethered loosely to the long anchor chains, at the mercy of the enormous seas.

The captain gathered his crew together on the poop deck. "This is what we'll do. I want Canso to take three seamen and lead a rope from the ship to shore. That way if the ship breaks up before we get everyone ashore, some people can go hand over hand to the beach. As soon as Canso and his men get ashore, Mr. Mckenzie will load the other boat with passengers. We'll run back and forth until everyone's safe. I'll stay on board ship to keep order. Now, Canso, who do you pick as your crew?"

The Nova Scotian seaman had no hesitation. "I'll take Georges, José and John. I'll need someone to play out the rope as we go to shore. Meg can do that."

"All right. Get your crew into the larboard boat. Mr. Ryerson, bring the two-hundred-foot rope that's in the storeroom."

The bosun and Tommy disappeared below as Canso's crew climbed into the whaler. Tommy and the bosun returned, dragging the heavy rope between them. With an effort it was pulled into the whaler and lay at Meg's feet. The captain had held onto one end of the rope and tied it with a hitch firmly around the mizzen-mast.

"Lower away!" said Canso, and the sailors on deck began lowering the boat with the hand winch.

On the way down, the commanding sailor shouted instructions to his crew. "When I shout 'starboard' or 'larboard' just pull those oars. Meg, you handle the tiller as well as playing out the rope."

A moment later and the boat was bobbing up and down in the waves, dangerously rubbing against the side of the ship. Canso unhooked the bow cable; Meg struggled to get the hook free at the stern. She chafed her hand; the sailors in the boat and on deck were wildly shouting instructions to her. Finally it came free. With a sudden surge of a wave the whaler was swept away from the ship and out into the open water.

Meg looked back at the *Scotian*. Hundreds of passengers lined the rail of the main deck anxiously watching their progress. On the poop deck the captain and crew seemed to be impulsively shouting instructions in spite of the fact that every word they said was swallowed by the driving winds. As she watched, a huge wave struck the *Scotian* and swept along her hull. The ship gave a sudden violent lurch as if the anchors were giving away. The sound of people on the deck screaming was heard by the sailors in the boat, but then the anchors seemed to hold.

The bow of the whaler was pointed toward the open sea. Canso waited for a wave to pass and then shouted, "Starboard oars!" John and Canso gave a strong pull. Meg fiddled with the tiller until she got it right. "Starboard!" Canso shouted again and the two seamen pulled with all their strength. Just as the boat was halfway around, a wave struck them broadside. For a moment it seemed like they might capsize, but the broad-beamed whaler held steady, and in the next instant they sunk down into the trough and righted themselves.

Meg had been working frantically to handle the tiller and play out the rope at the same time. As the whaler pointed toward shore, she pulled the tiller back into position and started throwing coils of rope over the side as fast as she could to give more slack.

"Pull!" Canso shouted and the four oars dipped in unison into the water. The whaler started to gain speed as they headed for shore. "Pull!" he shouted again to mark the rhythm of the oars. "Pull!" Just then a huge wave caught them, lifted the boat high into the air, and flung them toward the beach. "Pull!" and the boat leapt forward.

They could hear the pounding of the surf as they came closer to shore. "Pull!" Canso shouted. The crash of the breakers was all around them as the waves broke against rugged rock ledges and the shaley beach.

"Pull!" and the boat surged forward on a wave that broke into boiling foam.

For a moment they hesitated as the undertow pulled them back toward the sea and then, as the next wave broke, Canso shouted "Pull!" and the sailors put every ounce of muscle into the oars.

The crest of the wave broke around them and broke over the gunnels of the boat pushing them with a tremendous speed toward the shore. Suddenly the bow caught on a ledge and gave a lurch sideways, threatening to tip over and spill the sailors into the pounding surf.

In a second Canso was over the bow, thigh deep in the water, struggling with the enormous weight of the boat. As the wave began to slip back, he shouted to the others and they were into the icy cold sea, struggling to hold the boat from being dragged back into deep water. Only Meg remained, playing out the rope as fast as she could.

With the next wave the boat lifted up and over the ledge and the four sailors pushed with every ounce of strength. The water swept over John, but still he shoved against the boat until he could feel its hull scraping against the hard shale beach.

The next moment the wave began sweeping back, seizing the boy in its fierce undertow. He grasped desperately at the side of the boat but the wave sucked him back out to sea; his clothes were weighing him down; he could not hold on. "Canso!" he shrieked in terror.

In the next instant Canso's powerful hand clasped the boy's wrist. With enormous strength John was pulled out of the grip of the surf and thrown onto the shale beach.

"Heave!" Canso was shouting. "Heave!" But before the boy could get back to help, the three sailors had wrestled the heavy boat up onto the beach.

For a moment they collapsed, completely exhausted from their efforts. Then Canso was on his feet again. He leapt into the boat, picked up what remained of the coil of rope and with the help of the others began dragging it across the beach. When they had gone twenty yards they came to a big pine tree. Canso looped the rope around the trunk.

"We'll have to pull it as taut as possible," he shouted. The four sailors and Meg grasped onto the wet, heavy rope and with a signal from Canso they pulled with all their might. Again Canso shouted, and then again, until slowly the rope tightened. Finally the Nova Scotian sailor tied it firmly around the tree.

They ran back to the water's edge waving their arms to signal that the rope was secure. Just as they got back to shore they saw the *Scotian* lifted with an enormous wave; the anchors seemed to slip and the ship was pushed twenty feet toward shore. Suddenly the *Scotian* lurched over on her starboard beam and for an instant it seemed as if she was going to roll over until the masts were in the water. But, miraculously, the anchors held, the roll was stopped and the ship lay with a thirty-degree angle to starboard.

From the beach they could see the passengers running desperately from side to side of the deck and could imagine the panic and turmoil the unstable condition of the ship was producing.

Canso brought matches out from under his oilskins. "Make as big a fire as you can, Meg! We have no time to lose!"

CHAPTER 17

THE sailors waded up to their waists in the icy water, turning the whaler toward the sea. They waited until a wave broke around them, and then, at an order from Canso, they scrambled over the gunnels and into the boat. "Row," he shouted and the whaler shot ahead. The crest of the next wave tossed them high in the air, toward the beach, but with powerful strokes of the oars they swept back into deep water.

As they came around the stern of the *Scotian* to the starboard side, they found utter chaos. The ship was now on a thirty-five to forty degree list and the starboard main rail was almost under the water. Gradually she seemed to be turning so that the starboard beam was to the open sea and huge waves were coming at midships.

The main deck was teeming with wild passengers trying to get aboard the mate's boat. The captain was at the rail, revolver in hand, shouting at the top of his voice as he tried to impose some type of order. Already the mate had nearly thirty-five women and children in his boat but still others tried to scramble aboard. At last the mate pushed off.

They were dangerously overloaded. Children were crying; mothers clutched their families, and the sailors worked to turn their boat and head for shore. Just as they began turning, a huge wave caught them broadside and for a moment it seemed as if they would be swamped, but the crew held the boat steady. In the next moment they were being swept along with the waves toward the beach.

Canso waited until the mate's boat had gone; then he turned their whaler around so that the bow pointed toward shore and eased into the starboard rail. Captain Barnard was almost screaming. "Women and children! Women and children only!" There was great shoving as people tried to get aboard. "Wait your turn!"

Commands for order were futile. The passengers felt the ship was about to go under at any second and they were irrational in their efforts to escape. One young man pushed his way past the women. The captain levelled his revolver at him. "Stay back!" he threatened, but the man was almost in the boat now and others were pushing from behind. At the last moment Canso reached up and pushed the man with such force that he was heaved back on the deck.

The whaler bobbed up and down dangerously, rubbing against the hull of the ship with every wave. In the loading, more than one person fell into the sea and had to be pulled out. Now the boat was crowded. Women and children were squeezed tightly onto seats and crouched on the floor of the boat which sloshed with inches of cold sea water.

Canso searched the deck for Peggy Laing and finally found her at the back of the crowd trying to help an older man who appeared to be injured. The powerful sailor shouted for her to get on board the boat, but with a firm shake of her head she refused.

"Cast off!" ordered the captain and the next moment they were drifting free.

"Pull!" shouted Canso and the whaler began heading for shore.

As they rounded the stern of the ship they could see that the mate's boat was in trouble. It was at the beach half-filled with water. Women and children were in the surf struggling against the huge waves.

"Pull hard!" Canso shouted and their whaler shot ahead with extra speed. Just as they got to the beach a huge wave lifted them up on its crest and hurled the boat with tremendous momentum up on the rocky beach.

Canso led the sailors and some of the women across the beach to the floundering boat. Women and children were being flung about in the waves. Canso seemed to hurl people toward shore and then go back for more. Meg was in the water up to her waist and John was forcing his way through a breaker to help two children caught in the fierce undertow.

Some would surely have been lost had other people not arrived. Already there were half a dozen Nova Scotian villagers who had spotted the shipwreck and had come on foot to give assistance.

There was no time to lose. People were wet and cold; women and children were sobbing wildly. Meg and the villagers took command and led them to the blazing bonfire that burned on the beach. The sailors turned the mate's boat on its side to empty out the water and then the two whalers set back out to the ship again.

Canso's boat arrived at the *Scotian* first. The ship was in a dangerous position. The anchors were not holding. Slowly she was being pushed against an underwater shelf and was turning so the starboard beam faced the open sea. The storm blew enormous waves directly onto shore, pounding against the exposed starboard rail, threatening to crush the ship at any moment.

Again the captain imposed his will by threats with his revolver. This time the load was mostly women. Again Canso searched desperately for Peggy, and shouted for her to come, but again she firmly shook her head indicating that she would wait until the end.

Loading took less than a minute and they were back at sea again, pulling for the beach. They landed without mishap, unloading as quickly as they could, turning their boat around and heading back out to the ship.

Each time they returned to the ship they found her sinking further and further into the water. Already the main rail had submerged and people had to flee to the poop deck. As the whalers came in around the stern of the ship, the waves would smash them up against the deck, threatening to capsize them. As quickly as possible the passengers would leap aboard and they would set back to shore again.

Soon there were less than a hundred people clutching onto the larboard poop rail. The *Scotian* had slipped even more. Her tall masts were into the water, and the waves pounding in from the sea frequently smashed the decks with such force that they washed up and over the hulk of the ship. Canso realized they would have to take as many as they could, because it was unlikely she would remain afloat for long.

In order to load, the people had to slide down the deck and into the whaler. Many ended in the water and had to be pulled over the gunnels and into the boat, but quickly they were filled. Peggy Laing was still there, the last woman aboard. She wanted to stay until the end in case someone needed her help, but Canso was furious and ordered her to come. She ignored him. Finally he stood up on the seat of the whaler, and grabbed at her arm. She struggled for a moment, but then seemed to realize that there was no point in staying aboard ship any more and allowed herself to be pulled into the boat.

They were crammed with fifty people as they pushed off. As they rounded the stern of the ship, they almost struck the mate's boat as he was coming in to take off the last group of people. "Row!" Canso shouted and his crew pulled on their oars, their muscles straining with the exertion. It seemed for a moment as if they were going to flounder but the next wave picked them up and pushed them toward shore. With two more powerful strokes they were on the beach.

Canso, John and the other sailors waited for the mate's boat to bring the last load. It seemed to take a long time but finally the whaler rounded the stern of the *Scotian*. They were loaded to the gunnels. Carefully they made their way to the beach, taking advantage of every wave. As they arrived there was the joy of deliverance shining in the passengers' faces.

But as their whaler touched bottom the mate began shouting to Canso and his crew. "It's the cap'n! He refused to come!"

For a second the crew stood as if stunned by the news. Then, with sudden decisiveness, Canso shouted, "To the boat!" and ran with José, Georges and John toward their whaler. A moment later they had ridden through the pounding surf and were rowing recklessly toward the sinking ship.

The *Scotian* had sunk deeply into the sea now, threatening to go under at almost any moment. As each wave struck against the deck it sent an enormous shower of water into the air. It seemed as if at any moment the ship would be crushed and break into a thousand pieces.

The sailors leaned with all their force into their oars until finally they rounded the ship's stern. The *Scotian* was completely on her side now and three-quarters of her hull had sunk into the water. The masts were submerged except for the yardarms that poked like dead branches out of the water. The sailors were careful not to bring the whaler too close to the hull, but slowly they eased in against the poop deck, trying to keep a few feet away so they would not be smashed by the huge waves.

The captain was nowhere to be seen. John and Canso both stood up in the boat, searching the deck and the sea for a human shape, while Georges and José kept the boat steady.

"There he is!" John shouted. "He's midships, over there." Captain Barnard was clutching the rail, half in and half out of the water. He seemed to be trying to make his way, hand over hand, to the nearly submerged forward section of the ship. He was still wearing the jacket with brass buttons and his captain's hat.

"Cap'n Barnard!" Canso shouted. "Cap'n!" But the wind and waves carried away his voice and the captain gave no sign of recognition.

"Captain!" John shouted at the top of his voice. "Captain, come back!" The boy looked at the others. "What can he be trying to do?"

"I don't know," said Canso. "Wait here. I'm going for him." A moment later the Nova Scotian sailor scrambled over the bow of the whaler and made his way along the poop rail.

"I'm coming too!" John shouted and, in spite of the protests from the other sailors, he followed Canso.

The deck of the *Scotian* was lying broadside and she was sinking rapidly. Each wave pounded with unrelenting fury, often sweeping right over the deck and onto the other side. As the two sailors struggled after their captain, the waves battered their bodies up against the deck.

As they got to the poop rail Canso shouted, "Cap'n! Cap'n!" but their master was close to the foredeck now and either did not hear or chose to ignore them. They struggled on through the refuse of broken casks, each foot taking them farther and farther away from the boat, their only means of escape. Canso pulled himself along, closing the gap between himself and the officer. "Cap'n, stop! We have no time to lose!"

Captain Barnard finally turned toward them. His eyes stared wildly as he cried out, "Keep back! The two of you. Keep back!" He waved his arm in their direction and in his hand was the black shape of the revolver.

"Where are you going, Cap'n?"

"I've got to be sure that everyone's ashore, Canso."

"They are ashore, Cap'n. We are the only ones left aboard ship."

"I've got to be sure, Canso. Don't you see? I am the captain. I am responsible." John glanced at Canso. How would they ever be able to get this big man through the sea and back to the boat if he fought against them?

"They are all ashore, Cap'n," Canso pleaded. "We must abandon ship." He made a motion as if he was going to move forward.

"Keep back. I'll shoot!"

"Please, Cap'n."

"I've got to be sure. I am responsible."

A huge wave pounded them against the deck. The *Scotian* rolled up, and then, when the wave receded, sunk even deeper.

"We've got to go back, Cap'n."

"Keep away, I'll shoot! I must check my ship. My responsibility. I am the captain. No one must die."

John worked his way in front of Canso. "Captain Barnard!" he shouted. "It's John Bains. You must help me, Captain. You promised my sister Meg and I when we left Québec that you would get us back to Canada safely. You promised us, Captain. You must help me get to shore. It's your responsibility!"

The captain seemed to pull himself together. "Yes, boy. I'll help you … "

"Put your hand on my shoulder, Captain."

"Responsibility ... my responsibility," muttered the captain, looking past the men and down into the sea, where half of his ship lay submerged under the icy green water. Further out, the barren yardarms stuck out of the ocean. "I've lost her. She's gone under. But no one must die, do you hear?"

John moved slowly over the slippery deck toward the captain, hoping that his own face did not show any fear.

"No one is dead ... it's all right," he said, in a gentle, soothing voice. "But now you must help me and Canso get back to shore."

"My responsibility...."

"*We* are your responsibility," John said softly. He smiled encouragement at the captain who was beginning to nod his head in agreement. Very carefully, John reached for the gun and took it from the captain's hand. The captain did not resist. In fact, he did not even seem to notice that John had taken the gun, but stood there as if he were a child waiting to be told what to do.

"You are the captain of the *Scotian*," John reminded him. "You have a duty to your crew."

"Yes ... of course ... don't worry, John, I'll help you out." The captain squared his shoulders and adjusted his cap, looking more like his old self. "I know my duty."

"Well, then, put your hand on my shoulder and help me."

Cautiously, the men started back toward the boat, John in the lead, his heart thumping with relief and the captain's gun safely in his pocket. Captain Barnard followed, with his trembling hand on the boy's shoulder, and Canso close behind him. The waves pounded at their bodies and they had to pull themselves hand over hand along the rail. Finally they made it up to the poop deck, and then, with great effort, dragged themselves into the whaler. The waves smashed their boat against the nearly submerged deck, but José and Georges managed to push away from the ship and out into deep water.

As their boat surged onto the shore, John heard a sigh go up from the crowd on the rocky beach. He leapt quickly onto the beach, and turned to see the top of the *Scotian's* royal yardarm slowly sinking beneath the frothy white waves. Then the part of the hull that was still above water gave a sudden lurch and began rapidly to go under. There was a loud groaning noise, as trapped air in the *Scotian*'s hold began to empty out. Now there was only a portion of the starboard rail to be seen above the ocean, and then it, too, disappeared, and there was no sign the *Scotian* existed, except the seagulls circling over the place where she had wrecked, and the tangled ropes, kegs, furniture, foodstuffs and spars being swept ashore by the pounding surf.

John stood motionless for a moment on the littered beach; then he turned and saw that Meg, Peggy Laing, the Captain and Canso were standing beside him. Canso's head was bowed, and the captain suddenly looked very old and very tired, the madness now gone from his face. He turned to John, and the boy saw that there were tears streaming from his eyes.

"I pushed her too hard," the captain said quietly. "I should have taken more care."

"Never you mind, Captain," Canso said, clapping him on the shoulder. "In a way, it's better she's gone."

"How can you say that?" asked the captain, astonished. "I have nothing now. No money, no cargo, nothing. My life's work is at the bottom of the sea."

"I say it's for the best," Canso insisted. "You're a ship's captain, not a businessman. You can hire yourself out to another company and be a sailor again."

"Right back where I started."

"And better for you. Owning that ship was driving you to madness."

"Ridiculous," the captain snorted, looking offended. But slowly a faint smile began to cross his face. "You may have a point, Canso, about taking another command. I still have my captain's papers, after all."

Canso took the master by the arm and steered him up toward the beach. "Come on. Let's go and talk to the people who turned out to help us, and find out where we are in Nova Scotia." He turned to Peggy and with a broad smile offered her his other arm. Then the three of them — the master, the young woman and the sailor — walked up the beach toward a huge bonfire. Only John and Meg now remained by the whaler, looking out to spot where the *Scotian* had sunk.

"I thought I hated that ship," Meg said thoughtfully. "But I know that I'll miss her."

The wind from the sea was getting colder but still John and Meg lingered on the beach, depressed at the thought of leaving behind all the friends they had made on the voyage. Then Canso was standing beside them, smiling and motioning them to go up to the bonfire, his face happier than they had ever seen it.

"Come on, you two, there's hot tea and chowder, and Tommy has saved his accordion from drowning. My home town of Canso, the town that gave me my name, is close by. Peg and the captain are joining me there. If you want to come you'd be welcome."

He took them both by the hand, and immediately the two of them felt better. Laughing, John and Meg raced Canso up the beach to the bonfire, where Tommy had wrung the saltwater from his accordion and was starting up a true Nova Scotian seaman's shanty.

GLOSSARY OF NAUTICAL TERMS

ABLE SEAMAN: A trained sailor.

AFT: The stern or rear portion of the ship.

BALLAST: Anything heavy carried in the hold of a vessel to give stability. In the days of sailing this was usually rock.

BAROMETER: An instrument for measuring atmospheric pressure. When the barometer falls, it means bad weather.

BARQUE: A three- or four-masted vessel carrying square-rigged sails on her forward masts and fore-and-aft sails on her mizzen mast.

BEAM: 1. The width of the vessel. 2. Timbers used to support the deck in the construction of a ship.

BEFORE THE MAST: To be employed as a sailor on a ship.

BETWEEN-DECKS: (Usually pronounced 'tween decks.) Term used for the compartments below deck, but above the bilge.

BILGE: The lower part of the vessel's hold.

BILGE WATER: The stagnant water that lies in a vessel's hold.

BINNACLE: The case near the helm that encloses the compass.

BOSUN: (Sometimes known as "boatswain.") The officer aboard ship usually responsible for the deck crew.

BOW: Forward section of the ship.

BOW PORTS: Openings in the forward end of the ship used primarily to load and unload timber.

BRIG: A two-masted vessel carrying squared sails on each mast.

BRIGANTINE: A two-masted vessel with squared sails on the forward mast and fore-and-aft-rigged sails on her mainmast.

BRITISH NORTH AMERICAN SHIP: A vessel built in Eastern Canada.

BUOY: A floating marker, anchored to warn of shoals or to mark a channel.

CAPSTAN: A large spool-shaped cylinder, usually on the foredeck of a vessel, which is revolved by sailors turning it with bars or poles. In this way the rope or cable is wound around the capstan. It is used to lift the anchor or to move heavy loads.

COMBER: A big wave.

CRIMP: A person who gets men to serve as sailors by force or trickery. Crimps were particularly common in ports where there was a shortage of labour, such as Québec City and San Francisco.

CRINKLE: A loop of rope at the edge of a sail used for attaching ropes to tie down a sail.

DONKEY: A small portable steam engine used in the nineteenth century for loading vessels.

DOWNEASTERS: An American ship from the New England States.

DUFF: A flour dumpling boiled in water.
FORE: The front part or bow of the ship.
FORE-AND-AFT-RIGGED SAILS: Sails set lengthwise to the vessel, from the bow to the stern, rather than crosswise, such as square-rigged sails.
FORECASTLE: (Pronounced fo'c's'le.) The front part of a merchant ship where the sailors had their quarters.
FOREDECK: The deck at the foreward part of the ship. On most merchant ships the foredeck was raised above the maindeck.
FOREMAST: The mast nearest the bow of the ship.
FORETOP: A platform part of the way up the masts.
GALLEY: The ship's kitchen.
GUNNEL: The upper edges or sides of a boat or ship.
HALYARDS: Ropes used to set and trim sails.
HANDS: A term used for sailors aboard ship.
HARDTACK: A type of unleavened bread made in large wafers. This was part of the regular fare for seamen for several centuries.
HELM: The wheel or tiller by which a ship is steered.
HELMSMAN: The man who steers the ship.
HOLD: The interior of the ship below decks. The part of the ship where the cargo is carried.
HULL: The frame or body of the vessel which floats in the water.
INWARD BOUND: The direction of a vessel sailing into port.
IRONS: Chains and shackles used to hold a prisoner. To put a sailor in irons was a common disciplinary

procedure used aboard ships up to the turn of the century.

JIBS: Small triangular sails at the front of the ship rigged between the foremast and the jib boom.

JIB BOOM: The spar projecting beyond the prow of the ship.

KNOTS: A measurement of the rate of speed of a vessel. One knot is slightly more than one mile per hour.

LARBOARD: The left hand side of the ship when facing the bow. Modern terminology is "port."

LIME-JUICERS: English vessels. Named because of the British custom of serving lime juice to avoid scurvy during long voyages.

LOG: 1. An instrument dragged behind the vessel to determine its speed. 2. The journal kept by the captain which records the important events of the voyage.

LONGSHOREMAN: Another term for stevedore. A person who works at unloading and loading ships.

LUFFING THE SAILS: To turn the ship towards the wind so that the wind spills out of the sails. This makes it easier for the sailors to reef or stow the canvas.

MAINMAST: The principle mast of a vessel. In a square-rigged ship, the second mast from the bow.

MARLINESPIKE: A long tapered metal spike carried by sailors to open the strands of rope or cable when splicing.

MASTER: Another term for captain.

MATE: An officer of a merchant ship ranking below the captain.

MICKEY FINN: A drug, usually mixed with liquor, which can make a person unconscious.

MIDSHIPS: The middle of the vessel.

MIZZEN SAIL: The fore-and-aft sail on the mizzenmast

MIZZENMAST: The mast closest to the stern of the ship.

MOORINGS: The ropes and cables used to hold a ship when at a wharf.

OILSKINS: Waterproof coats and leggings worn by sailors in wet weather. They are made out of material waterproofed by treatment with oil.

ORDINARY SEAMAN: The rank of sailor below able seaman.

OUTWARD BOUND: The direction of the vessel leaving port.

PALM: A piece of leather worn on the palm of the hand by sailors when they were sewing sails. It was used to push the needle through the canvas.

PEAVEY POLE: A five-foot-long pole with a metal tip and a hinged iron hook on the end used to grasp and roll logs.

PILOT: A person licensed to steer vessels in and out of harbour or through difficult waters.

POOL: Some harbours, where currents and tides were particularly treacherous, developed a system of protective basins where ships could be moored. These basins came to be called pools.

POOP DECK: The raised deck at the stem of the vessel. It provides the roof for the officers' cabins.

POOPED: To receive a wave over the stem of the ship.

PROW: The forward part of the ship.

QUAY: A wharf, usually of concrete or stone.
RATLINE: Small, thin pieces of rope which join the shrouds of a ship and serve as a ladder for climbing into the rigging.
REEFING SAILS: To reduce the area of the sail exposed to the wind by tying part of it down.
RIGGING: The ropes and chains used for supporting and working the sails on a vessel.
RUNNING BEFORE THE WIND: Sailing with the wind behind the ship.
RUNNING RIGGING: All the movable parts of the ship's rigging.
SCHOONER: A vessel with two or more masts rigged in fore-and-aft fashion.
SCUPPER: An opening in the vessel's side which allows the water to run off the deck.
SHANGHAI: To kidnap sailors by drugging or other underhanded methods for service aboard ship.
SHIP: In the nineteenth century the term "ship" was usually reserved for a three-or-more masted vessel with square-rigged sails on all masts.
SHROUDS: Ropes stretching from the rail to the foretop used to support the masts and as ladders to climb up to work the sails.
SOUTHWESTER: (Pronounced sou'wester.) A sailor's waterproof hat made of oilskin.
SPLICE: To join ropes by weaving together the end strands.
SQUARE-RIGGER: A vessel with square sails.
STANDING RIGGING: The part of the rigging, such as the stays, which is set up permanently. In the

latter part of the nineteenth century, standing rigging was made out of thin, strong cable.

STARBOARD: The right side of the ship when facing the bow.

STERN: The rear end of a ship or boat.

STEERAGE: The section of the passenger ship occupied by those paying the lowest fare.

STEVEDORE: Another term for longshoreman. A person employed at loading and unloading vessels.

TACKING: To change the course of a ship in a zig-zag fashion so as to travel against the wind.

TIMBER DROGHER: An archaic term used for the vessels specializing in hauling timber.

TONNAGE: A measurement indicating the carrying capacity of a ship. It is used to indicate the ship's size.

WHALER: A large, long rowboat pointed at both ends. Often this design was used for lifeboats.

WINCH: A small device operated by turning a hand crank which is used to tighten ropes or to lift heavy weights.

WINDJAMMER: A large sailing ship.

YARD: A spar fastened at right angles across a mast to support a sail.